Paris Travel Guide

*Best Things to Do and See. Essential
Tips for First-Timers in Paris*

By Juliette Bellamy & Francesco Umbria

Table of Contents

Introduction

Paris: say the name of this unforgettable city, and the mind's eye is immediately filled with iconic images, from the Eiffel Tower to Notre Dame to the grandest museum in the world, the Louvre. It is inseparably associated with romance, with numerous films attesting to the City of Lights appeal to lovers. Its history is magnificent, from the Middle Ages to the present day, and it cultivates a lifestyle saturated with art and literature, culture, and leisure like no other city in the world. It is simply a singular place to visit.

From the emblematic Eiffel Tower to the treasures housed in the Louvre, Paris has plenty of must-see sites for everyone.

The Champs-Elysees Boulevard, bustling with shops and cafes and emanating sophistication and style, is the backbone of Paris, anchored by the Arc de Triomphe at one end and the Place de la Concorde at the other. The neighborhoods of Le Marais and Montmartre possess a unique charm all their own, while the ethnically diverse and exciting Latin Quarter never disappoints. Running through the center of Paris is the mighty Seine River, lifeblood of the city from ancient times to today, with the Ile de la Cite sitting gloriously in the middle of Parisian life.

With this guide, you will discover much about all of these sites and more, from how to get off the tourist path to what you should do if you plan to have an extended visit. You will also find, at the end of the book, a thorough list of practical considerations that will help you plan the best, most memorable trip you can imagine. So, take down your suitcases and scour your calendar: you're about to embark on the trip of a lifetime. Bon voyage!

Chapter 1:

Why Visit Paris? The Top 10 Most Loved Reasons

Any romantic who dreams of travel must necessarily dream of Paris: it is one of the most remarkable cities in the world, famed for its romance, for its food, for its sights, and for its unique quality. There is no other city in the world quite like it. From the monumental (the Eiffel Tower, the Louvre museum) to the charming (the art deco signs to the Metro, the street cafes), Paris offers a cornucopia of sights and sounds, experiences and entertainment to delight any visitor.

There are any number of iconic cities throughout the world that offer their own special brands of atmosphere and excitement — Venice with its canals, Honolulu with its luaus, and so on — but Paris has always proven itself to be one of the most popular destinations on any continent.

It has survived much in its fascinating history; it has been home to revolutions and enlightenments, ideas and science; it boasts some of the most recognized structures and monuments in the world. In short, not many people would fail to include it on a so-called "bucket list," and the fact that, in the 21st century, this ancient city still continues to offer more and more for any traveler means that it continues to hold its eternal appeal.

You might not expect the variety of options that Paris has to offer — aside from the greatest hits like the Eiffel Tower and the Louvre — but it has so many different sites and activities for the local and the tourist alike.

Aside from those greatest hits, you have medieval neighborhoods, cobblestone streets, ethnic culture that goes back centuries.

There is something to see and something to learn around every corner. This is why a thorough guide to the city is so important: you want to make absolutely sure that you don't miss out on anything. While you can go for just a few days and have a memorable experience, planning for more will allow you to truly experience one of the greatest cities on earth.

A first-time visitor might be overwhelmed by the sheer variety of options offered by the city, but there will always be those must-see destinations that appear on any list about the City of Lights. This guide will give you a thorough overview of many of them, but there are always more to be explored. As each individual will have his or her own Top 10, and as Paris has many more than ten top experiences, this guide divides the Top 10 list via the categories below. Within each category are a plethora of reasons to love Paris and gives every visitor the ability to customize their own must-see list. Having said that, the chapter will end with the ultimate Top 10 list, with the most popular attractions and destinations detailed for any traveler, from the first timer to the savvy returner. The chapters that follow will detail some of the most loved reasons, as well as give practical advice on traversing the city and exploring the best the city has to offer. Bon voyage!

Sights

The beauty and distinctiveness of Paris is unparalleled, and among the many pleasures of traveling there is to soak in the unique ambiance. From the art deco Metro signs to the broad boulevards and meandering alleyways, Paris is a city you can literally lose yourself in. The sights of any particular city mark its character and reveal its history. Paris not only has its own particular geographic look with its layout along the winding Seine River, but it also boasts home to a number of incredibly distinctive landmarks that all travelers know even before arrival.

No view of Paris would be complete without the distinctive and magnificent outline of the famed Tour Eiffel, the nineteenth-century marvel of engineering and artistic achievement. Controversial at first, the **Eiffel Tower** has since become an icon of the city and is currently the most visited monument in the world. In addition, it is the tallest structure in Paris and is thus visible throughout the city, one of the unavoidable if wholly welcome sights that loom large in the City of Lights.

Certainly, nobody should visit Paris without a trip to the **Louvre** museum. Housing some of the greatest masterpieces in history, the Louvre contains paintings and sculptures, archeological pieces and historical finds. From the infamous Louvre Pyramid — another controversial structure — out front to the treasures within, the Louvre houses copious wonders.

Another landmark of Paris, the **Notre Dame** Cathedral, is almost always at the top of a traveler's list when visiting. Alas, Our Lady of Paris was recently and quite severely damaged by fire in the summer of 2019, so it is currently under reconstruction and will not be open to the public for quite some time. Nevertheless, she remains steadfast and somber, keeping watch over the Ile de Cite as she has since the twelfth century. She is still worth a look and a tribute.

Historical Sites

In addition to the lovely look of the city, Paris is also home to many landmarks of historical significance. These sites remind us of the role that Paris has played in the history of France and in the history of Europe and the world.

Perhaps the most well-known of these historical sites is the **Arc de Triomphe**. Erected at the end of the glamorous Champs Elysees in 1806, the ornate arch is a tribute to the military victories of France throughout the ages, particularly by Napoleon. Like Napoleon himself, the arch is a larger than life structure with engravings in images and words to tell the story of France's greatness. Whatever the historical judgment on the actions of Napoleon, he did leave behind this bold monument recognizable to all who visit Paris.

If you are a history buff, particularly of military history, then **Les Invalides** is another must-see site. Built in the 17th century by King Louis XIV, Les Invalides was originally intended to be a hospital for wounded soldiers and veterans. Today it houses a military museum, Musee de l'Armee, and contains the tomb of Napoleon himself. Expanded from its original building and purpose, Les Invalides is now a sprawling complex of various museums and offers numerous tours to travelers interested in the history and culture of France.

Another site of historical note is the **Place de la Concorde**. This plaza has been significant from the time of the French Revolution until the present day. Originally the site of the notorious executions by guillotine of Louis XVI and his infamous wife, Marie Antoinette, it is now dedicated to the preservation of peace and harmony post-Revolution. Its location is marked by the great Luxor Obelisk, a pillar that was given to France by Egypt in the 19th century. The Obelisk is an ancient artifact that was once found at the entrance to the Luxor tomb in Egypt.

Smells

As Marcel Proust so eloquently reminisces in his masterwork *In Search of Lost Time*, just the smell of a simple madeleine cookie can take him back to his childhood and another world. Smell is perhaps the most intricate trigger of memory and love, and Paris itself is imbued with its own particular scents to keep us longing for it far after we have left.

If there were a food of the city, it would clearly be the **baguette**. Slim and elegant, with a crackly crust and an airy crumb, baguettes can be had from just about any shop in the city. In the mornings, the air is filled with the smell of baking bread, and Parisians start their day with a strong cup of coffee and a bit of baguette or croissant. While some lament that the traditional bakeries are dying out due to industrialized production, Paris still boasts some of the best bread and bakery products in the world. The early morning scent of baking bread filling the air is as Parisian as the Eiffel Tower.

Let us not also forget one of France's most distinguished cultural contributions to the world: **wine**. Savoring a lovely plate of France's many cheeses alongside a glass of red or white wine is clearly a must for any tourist. Swirling the wine, inhaling its aromas, will give you a sense memory that you won't soon forget. In Chapter 11, you will find more discussion of the unique foods and wines of France.

Savories

Speaking of food and wine, France is famous for its culinary contributions to the world, of course, and Paris is no exception. Because it is the capital of France, Paris draws on all the food traditions that exist throughout the country, not to mention that it is a cultural melting pot, bringing people from all over the world together through food.

A particularly French tradition that exists to this day is the **café culture**: sitting in a café, sipping a coffee and watching passersby is a European habit that you can find in many cities. The French café is less formal than a restaurant and open all day long, so it caters to the peripatetic nature of the traveler. The brasserie is an extension of the café that typically specializes in beer as well as hearty cuisine; the bistro is the casual restaurant that ups the ante with the quality of food and, in contemporary Paris, can serve anything from traditional French dishes to the cuisine of Asia and Africa. Life is not necessarily slower in France, but the appreciation of good food, wine, and other drinks is considered a birthright.

One of the best places to check out the various traditional foods of France is on the **Rue Cler**. This particular street houses a variety of vendors selling everything from wine and cheese to charcuterie and fresh fruit and vegetables. Essentially an open-air market in the middle of the city, Rue Cler, is a necessary stop for anyone interested in the magnificent food of France.

The **Latin Quarter** is another place wherein a traveler can experience the food culture of Paris — though of a more distinctly modern kind. Named for the Latin speaking scholars who once thrived in this area, near the University of Paris, the Latin Quarter has become home to a plethora of immigrants from many different cultures. Thus, the food offerings hail from all over the world, particularly Greece and Africa, as the diaspora settles in this area. This is a good place to break out of your comfort zone and try something new.

Situations

Obviously, Paris has a lot to offer in the realm of experience in general, and the word "situations" describes some of the various scenarios in which you can find yourself exploring and doing. From shopping to dancing, Paris also has much to offer beyond its cultural and historical monuments and traditions.

Perhaps the most renowned boulevard in the world, the **Champs Elysees** offers a staggering array of high-end shops and cafes in order to satisfy any traveler's needs and desires. Spanning the distance between the Place de la Concorde to the Arc de Triomphe, a stroll along this boulevard is a necessary stop for any tourist, from landmark to landmark, from luxury to luxury. This is a shopper's paradise, to be sure.

Once home to the city's Jewish population, the neighborhood of **Marais** is known for its trendy restaurants and nightlife, as well as a thriving art scene.

This is the kind of neighborhood that you want to frequent as a regular, where the barman knows your drink.

Enjoy its less touristy vibe and take in some eclectic shopping while you're at it. You will also find the wonderful and quirky museum of art, the Pompidou Center, in the Marais district; if modern art is something you enjoy, this is not to be missed.

In the neighborhood of **Montmartre**, you will find the former haven for many artists and a bohemian lifestyle that is perhaps best represented by the famous cabaret, the **Moulin Rouge**. While it now attracts tourists and upwardly mobile young people, Montmartre was once the home to such luminaries as Claude Monet, Pierre-August Renoir, and Edgar Degas. Walk through the neighborhood to see the exteriors of houses belonging to these artists and others, like Picasso and Van Gogh, before taking in a show at the Moulin Rouge. Certainly, the show is expensive and bit kitschy, but it preserves a particular flair that this gritty neighborhood has always displayed.

Sensations

While Paris is full of sensational art, food, drink, and experiences, there are a couple of truly astounding and over-the-top sensations that you may wish to partake in. Not to everyone's taste, these sensations exhibit a spirit of excess and joie de vivre that encapsulates part of the French sensibility.

A quick day trip from Paris, the Palace of **Versailles** is worth the visit if you have the time. Built in the 17th century, Versailles represents the moment when France is the literal center of European culture—everyone spoke French and followed French fashion in everything from theater to art and beyond. Ornate, enormous, and over-the-top, the Palace of Versailles was once the center of government and the home of kings, most notably Louis XIV, known as the Sun King. The tour takes you through the three most spectacular parts of the campus, the Chateau or main palace, the intricately elaborate Gardens, and the Trianon Palaces. The tour can be quite crowded, so be sure to arrive early for the best experience.

For another spectacular sensation that won't take you out of the city itself, take a visit to the strikingly designed **Pompidou Center** in the Marais neighborhood. All of its internal workings—pipes and ducts, as well as the escalator—are prominently displayed on its exterior, with its bright primary colors. The greatest artists of Modern art are all on display here, as well: Picasso and Matisse, Kandinsky and Dali, as well as a lot of lesser-known artists working post-1960 are housed with the permanent collection. There are also always interesting traveling exhibits, as well as a coterie of street performers and other entertainment just outside the doors. It is one of the most sensational buildings—and exhibits—in all of Paris.

Scenes

Another reason to visit Paris resides in its cinematic history: we have all seen some of the most iconic scenes in some of the most iconic movies that take place in the streets and amid the buildings in Paris. Watch these films before you go to get a sense of the city from the theatrical point of view. Be sure to pay attention to where you are to catch a glimpse of what Leslie Caron was up to in *An American in Paris* or where Owen Wilson wandered in *Midnight in Paris*. These cinematic landmarks are sure to delight any moviegoer. Another more recent movie that acts as a love letter to the city is the charming independent film, *Paris, Je T'aime*. The heralded *Amelie* is another good film to prepare you for your own travels through Paris.

Stories

Not only is Paris rife with cinematic history, it is also resplendent with literary history, as well. Marcel Proust is one of the great homegrown French writers who lived and worked in Paris, but Paris became a notable retreat for a number of expatriate writers in the 1920s and 30s. Ernest Hemingway famously wrote much of his work there, most notably *A Moveable Feast*. Gertrude Stein and Alice B. Toklas hosted grand parties there, and some of America's most famous African American writers, Richard Wright and James Baldwin among them, chose Paris as their headquarters for a time.

Out of that rich literary heritage grew a cottage industry catering to writers and their ilk that continues to this day in the legacy of the **Left Bank booksellers**. Set up in stalls along the Seine River, these secondhand booksellers have been peddling wares in the area since Medieval times.

A brick-and-mortar store that is legendary in the area is **Shakespeare & Co. Bookstore**. Started by a young American, Sylvia Beach, back in the post-World War I years.

All of the American expatriate writers gathered here, and Sylvia Beach herself became a legend for publishing James Joyce's notorious *Ulysses*. It's worth a trip here to pay homage to all of these great names of the past.

Secrets

Paris is also home to some hidden gems: a museum overshadowed by the great Louvre, a church overshadowed by the great Notre Dame, and a secret unique to this bustling city that lies below ground.

While the Louvre is, of course, not to be missed, the **Musee de Orsay** should be among your top ten stops when traveling to Paris. It contains the most extensive collection of great works of artists like Manet, Monet, Van Gogh, Degas, Renoir, Gaugin, and Cezanne. Essentially, the Orsay picks up, timewise, where the Louvre leaves off, housing works from the mid-nineteenth century to the onset of World War I. It is literally wall-to-wall with masterworks from that era.

Another overshadowed landmark that is not to be missed is **Sainte-Chapelle**. This gothic cathedral has some of the most stunning stained-glass art in all of Europe, culminating in the famed Rose Window. Particularly now that Notre Dame is under reconstruction, Sainte-Chapelle really should not be skipped. Built in the 13th century, its beautiful gothic exterior and raised interior altar are sure to delight.

Finally, the City of Lights itself hides an interesting secret: **The Catacombs**. Underneath the city lies a crypt filled with the remains of about six million former citizens. In the late eighteenth century, Paris decided to empty the cemeteries and move the bones to these underground chambers in the interest of health and space. Stacked about five feet high and up to eighty feet deep, the somber piles of bones are both awe-inspiring and humbling.

The Seine

Last, there will be no need for you to look for this final site on this partial list: the **Seine River** dominates the geography and history of Paris entire, running for some 500 miles. In fact, Paris is a city of small islands, really, perched atop the mighty Seine, and its legendary prowess for romance is not to be underestimated. Be sure to take a nighttime stroll along the waterway, preferably under the light of a happy moon. Don't miss the Pont Neuf bridge: once the "new bridge," it is now the oldest in Paris, built around 1600. It spans the widest part of the river.

The Ultimate Top 10 List

The following sites are the ones that most experts deem absolutely necessary for any visit to beautiful Paris. Add to them any one of the sites and experiences described above, and you will have a trip to truly remember. They are as follows, in no particular order of greatness:

- ➤ The Eiffel Tower
- ➤ The Louvre Museum

- Notre Dame
- Champs Elysees
- Arc de Triomphe
- Sainte-Chapelle
- Musee de Orsay
- Montmartre in the 18th Arrondissement with Moulin Rouge
- Le Marais with Pompidou Center
- The Latin Quarter with its cultural diversity and the University of Paris

Chapter 2:

Best Time to Visit

Truly, any time is a grand time to visit one of the most beautiful and historic cities in Europe; however, any romantic will tell you that "Springtime in Paris" symbolizes the ideal dream trip for many people. It is the trip you often see illustrated in classic books and movies that have been made about Paris or in Paris.

Paris can be hot in the summer, cold in the winter, and rather lonely in the fall; on the other hand, Paris is the most crowded and the most expensive during the spring and early fall months.

Prices drop and crowds thin during summer and at the height of winter, so it truly depends on the individual traveler as to what time might be the best time for them. Any time you are able to go will be a memorable one, regardless. Below is a season by season breakdown of the advantages and disadvantages of traveling to and within Paris during different times of the year.

Spring

There are many advantages to traveling to Paris in spring: the weather is lovely, and there are interesting events and deals for tourists during that time. Beware, though, that many other people have the same notion of how romantic Paris is in spring, so it can be quite crowded. Still, with careful planning and preparation, a trip to Paris in spring comes with a host of potential advantages.

> ➤ The Night of Museums is held in May in Paris, wherein all of the major museums are open at night and free of charge. The exact date changes according to the year, so check with the tourism board for the particular date for that year. Obviously, the event is highly popular not just

with tourists but also with locals, so it can be crowded, but usually, the spirit is congenial and celebratory.

➤ The best time to celebrate France's café culture is undoubtedly spring when the weather is mild, and the people-watching is prime. Take up a table on the sidewalk and have a cup of coffee and a croissant; watch the world go by as you sit back in leisurely pleasure.

➤ Another advantage of visiting Paris in the spring is to take in the blooming gardens in all their unparalleled glory. This is the time to revel in the intricate workings of the city's many parks and gardens, among them the Garden of Plants, the Jardin des Tuileries, and the Parc Monceau. These are just a few of the many lovely public parks and gardens that Paris has to offer.

➤ This is also the time of year to take full advantage of outdoor markets, bursting with fresh produce and other local products. There are many throughout the city, catering to different tastes. If you are a so-called foodie, the Bastille, Marche Rue de Dejean, and Boulevard Raspail are among the best.

➤ Speaking of food, springtime in Paris is the perfect time for a picnic in the park—it's really such a cliché that it must be true. Pack a tote with a baguette, some cheese and charcuterie, some fresh strawberries, and a bottle of good wine and find a spot on the Champ de Mars in front of the city's most iconic monument, the Eiffel Tower.

- ➢ If you are a music lover, the festival Villette Sonique usually takes place at the end of May, bringing together indie rockers from all over Europe and beyond.
- ➢ Finally, the Easter season in Paris can be quite magnificent. This Catholic-dominated country celebrates Easter with almost all the fervor with which it celebrates Christmas (and the weather is, of course, nicer). Check with various cathedrals throughout the city to see if they are open to the public for mass. That's a souvenir without a price, for sure.

Summer

Paris can also be nice during the summer but do be forewarned that crowds can be overwhelming at times, the weather can get quite hot, and the month of August is fairly dead—many Parisians get out of the city for the entire month, leaving many businesses and attractions closed. The other deterrent to summer travel is that prices for flights, hotels, and other amenities rise during the height of tourist season. The earlier you book for a summer trip, the better you will be able to get relative bargains. And, although the weather does get quite warm, it doesn't usually climb into the 80s for very long. Paris is a rather temperate city, for the most part. There are some other advantages to traveling to Paris in June and July.

➤ There are numerous free outdoor events held throughout the Parisian summer: outdoor screenings of movies, concerts, and other festivals are usually free and open to the public. Look to tourism sites for information on dates and events or ask your concierge what's going on during your stay.

➤ Over a few weeks during the summer, city officials construct an artificial "beach" along the banks of the

Seine. Soak up the sunshine like a local while enjoying the sights and sounds.

> Don't forget Bastille Day! July 14 celebrates the establishment of the French Republic and is the nation's biggest holiday, rivaling the Fourth of July. July also sees the Tour de France.

Fall

Paris in fall gives you the advantage of fewer tourists in the city, so there is less crowding at attractions and better ability to snag reservations. The weather is still mild, much like spring, and the foliage is attractive even though not in full bloom. Prices begin to drop, as well, so this is a great time to travel if you're on a tight budget. There are also a handful of events during fall that you might want to schedule for or around.

> Paris Fashion Week is the last week in September, so unless you are a huge fashion buff (and have a lot of money or clout), you might want to avoid that week. Hotels and reservations can be hard to come by.

> There is also the impressive and ongoing Autumn Festival in Paris. Running from early September to

early December, this festival features art exhibits, film showings, theatre events, and musical concerts throughout the season and in various locations. Check official Paris tourist sites for specific dates and events.

➢ Paris also celebrates Armistice Day (what we call Veterans Day) in November.

Winter

Finally, Paris in winter can be wonderful, if cold and wet: December is typically the rainiest month in the city. Still, prices drop precipitously in the winter months (December through February) and thus can offer a respite to the budget-minded traveler. This also means that hotels are typically cheaper and easier to get, while reservations are also easy and lines for attractions are short. If you do decide to vacation in Paris during winter, December is the best time to see that the City of Lights truly lives up to its nickname.

➢ An ice-skating rink is erected in front of the Eiffel Tower for the holiday season, so you can take advantage of something that most tourists never get to experience.

➢ Shopping for the holidays explodes throughout the city, with markets popping up everywhere, not to mention the festiveness of the shops in general. Window displays compete for attention in colorful, sparkling variety.

➤ Holiday treats abound, from special pastries like sugar plum cakes to roasted chestnut vendors on the sidewalks.

➤ And, of course, the lights: Paris drapes itself in lights throughout the holiday season, from the glow of the Eiffel tower to the window displays to the magnificent holiday scene along the Champs Elysees.

Chapter 3:

The Eiffel Tower: Landmark of the City

Ah, the Tour Eiffel is truly one of the most enduring signifiers not only of Paris but also of France itself — one of the few landmarks that instantly evokes a particular city in a particular way. You need only show an image or mention the word "Eiffel" to evoke beautiful and romantic images of the City of Lights. Amazingly, this iconic structure was only intended to stay up for a couple of years — unimaginable today — and caused quite a bit of controversy during its initial tenure and beyond.

History, Controversy, and Embrace

The history of the Eiffel Tower is almost as interesting as the monument is enduring. Planned as an exhibit for the World's Fair in 1889, which Paris was hosting during the year of the centennial anniversary of the end of the French Revolution, the Eiffel Tower began construction work in 1887. Designed by Gustave Eiffel, in conjunction with engineers and an architect, the tower was originally conceived as an ornate structure with stained glass windows and an orb on top. Eventually, it was simplified into the structure we know today for reasons of cost and expediency. As one can imagine, building a nearly 1000-foot-tall structure during the late nineteenth century was no small feat: it took hundreds of workers — four workers were needed per each rivet fastened — in order to carry out the massive plan.

The tower was intended, of course, to awe the many spectators who would be coming from around the world to attend the World's Fair (there is no real modern equivalent to the World's Fair today; the closest approximation might be the Olympics).

The World's Fair was the time for nations to compete with one another, showing the sophistication of their culture and the worldliness of their capabilities. The construction of a towering structure of engineering brilliance was certainly one way in which Paris—and, by extension, France—could show off its might and talent to the world.

Gustave Eiffel was an entrepreneur and engineer who built various structures all over the world during his long career. The original vision for the Eiffel Tower was not his at all, ironically enough, and his name became attached to the project only after he had been persuaded that this would be a feat to put himself and France on the map, as it were, during the exhibition. Thereafter, he gave vast sums of money and reserves of energy to the daunting project.

His vision for the tower, in his own words, was that it would reveal "not only the art of the modern engineer, but also the century of Industry and Science in which we are living, and for which the way was prepared by the great scientific movement of the eighteenth century and by the Revolution of 1789, to which this monument will be built as an expression of France's gratitude."

Essentially, the Eiffel Tower is one of the culminating works of the Industrial Revolution and enduring symbol of the spirit that animated the nineteenth century, in general.

During the World's Fair, the reception of the tower was almost universally positive. In particular, one must note that it provided views of Paris that had heretofore never been seen — this was an age before airplanes, of course. At the time, it was also the tallest tower in the world, so it was irresistible as a beacon of modern engineering. Nearly two million people attended the fair, which ensured the immediate success of Eiffel and the company's creation.

It was also — amazingly — lit up at night with gas lamps encased in glass, with a beacon sending out beams of France's national colors (red, white, and blue) mounted near the top of the tower. Dignitaries and famous people from all over the world came to marvel at the sight. Not only was the tower an attraction in its own right, but it also housed four different restaurants for travelers to visit during the fair. Eiffel himself kept an office at the top tier of the tower, hosting visitors in his spare time — most notably, Thomas Edison.

Still, the reception wasn't universally positive: many prominent artists and other critics felt that the tower celebrated all that was mechanistic and unfeeling about the age, and the very values that Eiffel intended it to represent were the values that were under attack by those prominent artists. In short, the tower wasn't revered as a great work of art, but rather as a mechanical feat of engineering – which is what the designers intended, of course, but critics felt it overwhelmed the beauty of Paris instead of enhancing it. A vocal group of critics, including Paul Verlaine and Joris-Karl Huysmans, endorsed a written protest against the tower, reading in part as below:

"We come, we writers, painters, sculptors, architects, lovers of the beauty of Paris which was until now intact, to protest with all our strength and all our indignation, in the name of the underestimated taste of the French, in the name of French art and history under threat, against the erection in the very heart of our capital, of the **useless and monstrous** Eiffel Tower which popular ill-feeling, so often an arbiter of good sense and justice, has already christened the Tower of Babel. [...]

Is the City of Paris any longer to associate itself with the baroque and mercantile fancies of a builder of machines, thereby making itself irreparably ugly and bringing dishonor? To comprehend what we are arguing one only needs to imagine for a moment a tower of ridiculous vertiginous height dominating Paris, just like a gigantic black factory chimney, its barbarous mass overwhelming and humiliating all our monuments and belittling our works of architecture, which will just disappear before this stupefying folly.

And for twenty years we shall see spreading across the whole city, a city shimmering with the genius of so many centuries, we shall see spreading like an ink stain, the odious shadow of this odious column of bolted metal."

This protest could not be more strongly stated, one could argue, but as the tower neared completion and the resounding success of its presence during the World's Fair, views of its "monstrousness" began to soften.

Originally intended to stay up for only twenty years, changing world events ensured that the tower would last for much, much longer.

With the beginning of radio transmissions, the tower became of strategic importance; with its massive height, it could send and receive transmissions over great distances. With world war looming on the horizon, the tower began to be of military importance, as well. During the wars, the sight of the tower standing amid chaos came to symbolize the strength and resilience of the French people—and, thus, a temporary monument to celebrate the centennial of the French Revolution and display the greatness of France for a mere generation has now become the most enduring symbol of Paris and France today.

Practical Considerations and Fun Facts

> ➤ If you want to actually go up in the tower rather than just gaze upon it, be sure to book your tickets in advance. This can be done through any number of sites or through a travel agent, but it is a must if you intend to get in. There are different kinds of tickets for different experiences (such as booking for just second-floor access), as well as different pricing for different age groups. Do your research before you go and book in advance.

- It is an option to take the stairs from the ground floor to the second tier; if you wish to go all the way to the top, you must take the elevator, of course. But there are advantages to taking the stairs: you get to enjoy the view at your own pace, avoid the long lines for the elevators, and, of course, get some exercise.

- You can also make reservations at one of the two restaurants that are still operating at the Eiffel Tower. This means that you can skip the lines to get directly into the restaurant, though the menus are pricey, and the quality of the food is often hotly debated. Again, do your research and make the best choice for you and your traveling companions.

- Remember that, while the tower is beautiful and your experience is ultimately priceless, monuments and tourist attractions of any type will always attract thieves and others looking to prey upon relatively inexperienced tourists. Keep your belongings close to you: if you are a woman, wear your handbag strapped across your chest to discourage pickpockets and purse-snatchers; if you carry a backpack, be sure that it is securely fastened around you, rather than dangling off one shoulder. Just be alert and prepared, and you should be fine.

- Also remember to take your time: a rushed trip to one of the world's most visited monuments is a trip hardly worth taking. When planning your vacation, think about what is most important to you and always add extra time, just in case. If you simply wish to see the Eiffel Tower, its presence is ubiquitous throughout the city, of course. If you wish to engage more fully in the experience, plan accordingly and give yourself thoughtful time in which to do it. Remember that the Eiffel Tower at night is a potentially even more amazing—and romantic—experience. If you want to spring for a meal in the tower, then that might well be the right time to do it.

➢ If you do decide to visit the tower up close, keep in mind that there are other activities to do while you are in the area. First, if you don't want to book tickets—or forgot to do so in advance—you can always take a picnic lunch to have on the Champs de Mars at the foot of the grand tower. For people with disabilities or a fear of heights, this might be the ideal way to enjoy the iconic landmark.

➢ There are also boat cruises of the Seine that are offered around the tower, another way of getting up close to the monument without necessarily having to go up in it.

➢ Finally, there are other attractions in the area that might just be the nudge for you to make it worth the trek.

- The Rodin Museum is close by if you want to get an extra dose of culture. It houses many of the most impressive works by this famous sculptor, whose *Thinker* sculpture is perhaps the most famous of the twentieth century.

- Napoleon's tomb lies within the nearby Army Museum, which is located within the larger complex of the Hotel des Invalides. The museum also boasts detailed exhibitions concerning both world wars that are definitely worth seeing, especially if you or someone in your party is a history buff.

- There are also tours of the Paris sewer, amazingly enough, which trace the history of the sewers from Roman times through the medieval period up to the present day.

- Finally, there is the Mormottan Museum that is also nearby. It contains the most impressive collection of works by Claude Monet, who is considered the progenitor of the impressionist movement.

Chapter 4:

Champs-Elysees: The Most Famous Boulevard

Anchored by two of the most renowned landmarks in Paris, the Champs-Elysees is a glittering boulevard of retail dreams and historical glory. The finishing stop on the grueling Tour de France, this avenue is perhaps the most recognizable street anywhere in the world. Filled with elegant cafes and luxury shops, taking a stroll down the Champs-Elysees—the Elysian Fields of France—is a highlight of any traveler's visit.

Named for the Roman paradise for fallen heroes, the Champs-Elysees itself has an illustrious history. It has been in existence, in some form or another, since the early seventeenth century, acquiring its grand name at the beginning of the eighteenth century. Originally a garden path during the time of Louis XIV, the pathway became a boulevard lined with symmetrical elm trees over the years. As it developed, it grew in prominence, both because of its location and because of its growing beauty. It was often referred to as the "Grand Promenade." By the close of the eighteenth century, this was perhaps the most fashionable area in Paris, and the Champs-Elysees occupied a central role in the daily lives of wealthy Parisians.

Following the French Revolution, equestrian statues were added, and the park became a central point of celebration, as well.

During the early part of the nineteenth century, the park and boulevard were redesigned with cafes and a theater added: The Champs-Elysees was now becoming an entertainment hub. This was also the moment when the Place de la Concorde was designed and the Arc de Triomphe—the two major monuments that sit at either end of the boulevard—were commissioned.

The boulevard as we know it today was slowly being shaped by events and commerce. It would also serve as the site of many military parades, symbols of strength and victory along this most vital of avenues. By the 1920s, the avenue was the epitome of global elegance that is still its most enduring legacy.

Today, the Champs-Elysees hosts a number of retail outlets, trendy cafes, and glamorous nightclubs. Not only is it the finishing place for the internationally renowned Tour de France but it is also the home for the annual Bastille Day – the celebration of the end of the French Revolution – celebration and parade. As well, it has hosted some of the most triumphant parades in French history, with the end of World War I in 1919 and after the liberation of the city near the conclusion to World War II. The Champs-Elysees is truly the backbone of this meandering city.

Alas, the internationalization of the boulevard has been alarming to many and has arguably damaged its uniquely Parisian feel and reputation.

Various global brands were eventually allowed onto the avenue, which both lessened its appeals to luxury as well as its innate French-ness.

A Gap, Abercrombie & Fitch, and Starbucks now share space along the avenue with Louis Vuitton, Guerlain, and other iconic French brands. The intrusion of a McDonald's on the famed avenue was perhaps the worst blow to its prestige; however, that particular McDonald's happens to be one of the most profitable in the entire world. Thus, the Champs-Elysees still yet thrives in an age of globalization, and the merchant's association works to try to preserve its quality as much as possible given these external forces.

The reason for a stroll down the avenue is as much about absorbing a Parisian experience and outlook as it is about shopping. Bookended by monuments and serving up luxury and atmosphere in great dollops, the Champs-Elysees feels like a bustling business district, a fantasia of fashion, and an archaic sense of style while out for shopping. You can virtually picture the ladies who lunch in hats and gloves. It's an elegant place for nostalgia, some perfume, and a delicious meal or snack. In addition, you will want to check out the two famous monuments that sit at each end of the boulevard.

At one end, near the Rue Royale, sits the Place de la Concorde. This plaza has held a prominent spot in French history from the time of the French Revolution until the present day.

While it was originally the site of the notorious executions by guillotine of Louis XVI and his infamous wife, Marie Antoinette, it is now dedicated to the preservation of peace and harmony in the Republic of France. Its location is marked by the great Luxor Obelisk, an engraved pillar that was given to France by Egypt in the 19th century. The Obelisk itself is around 3000 years old and was once used to mark the entrance to the Luxor Tombs. So many Egyptian artifacts that are seen in the West are marked by controversy — were they looted? — that it's a happy change to see one that was gifted in a gesture of diplomacy.

At the other end of the Champs-Elysees sits the Arc de Triomphe, the famous arch commissioned by Napoleon after his victory in Austerlitz, but it was not completed until after his disgrace and deposition.

Erected in 1806, the ornate arch is a tribute to the military victories of France throughout the ages, particularly by Napoleon. Like Napoleon himself, the arch is a larger than life structure — the largest of its kind in the world — with engravings in images and words to tell the story of France's greatness.

Whatever the historical judgment on the actions of Napoleon, he did leave behind this bold monument recognizable to all who visit Paris. Below the arch rests the Tomb of the Unknown Soldier, where every day new flowers are placed, and the torch is lit. You need only be there at 6:30 each evening to see this ritual.

Obviously, there is no specific reservation to be made to enjoy the Champs-Elysees and all it has to offer. The following is a partial list of what is available on the boulevard, though these offerings do change over time, of course.

> ➢ Clearly, one of the main draws of Champs-Elysees is still the shopping, regardless of how international and potentially low-brow some of that shopping has become. If you look past some of the big international brands, there are some distinctive French shops to give you a sampling of a more authentic Parisian spirit:
>
>> o Longchamp, with their iconic Le Pliage bags, is one such stop.
>> o Lacoste, with its ever-popular crocodile logo, is also available here.
>> o There is Petit Bateau for lingerie needs
>> o Eric Bompard's famous cashmere sweaters.

- o Don't forget to make time for the Louis Vuitton store along the boulevard: even if you don't intend to buy (or can't possibly afford to buy) anything here, the store itself is a kind of landmark, a museum to fashion and this iconic French brand. It will make you feel elegant and accomplished just to walk through the doors.
- o There is also the famous French perfumery, Guerlain, with its high-end scents—this is the mason that created Shalimar—and wares. A small restaurant also resides in the three-story shop, where chefs prepare meals inspired by the scents in the store.
- o And if you are in the mood for some jewelry or a nice watch, stop into Cartier or Maboussin.

- ➢ In addition to shopping, the Champs-Elysees offers a number of dining and entertainment opportunities: Fouquet's is the most luxurious (and expensive) of the dining opportunities along the avenue, and its glamorous history makes it a destination spot. Hosting celebrities of all varieties throughout its more than 100-year history, Fouquet's is the place to see and be seen along the Champs-Elysees.
- ➢ There are also several Michelin-starred restaurants along the avenue, such as L'Atelier Etoile by famed chef

Joel Robuchon and Ledoyen, another upscale eatery. L'Alsace serves the famed choucroute from the German-adjacent region of France, and Flora Danica has jumped onto the Scandinavian cuisine bandwagon.

➤ If you'd like to go more casual (though perhaps not as casual as *McDo's*) or just need a snack, there is an outpost of Laduree which is famous for its macarons or 86 Champs, a new concept store which is an intriguing mash-up between Pierre Herme and L'Occitane.

➤ When seeking out nightlife and entertainment, the Champs-Elysees also has much to offer—though much of it is very upscale and expensive. Try the Lido cabaret show for a full-on entertainment spectacle or grab a seat at one of the bars along the boulevard, Planches or the Duplex or Raspoutine, among others. The only casino in Paris, the Paris Elysees Club, is also located here if you enjoy a little gambling.

➤ Finally, don't forget about the Grand Palais and the Petit Palais. Former palaces and residences, these remarkable buildings now house various exhibitions. Check updated tourism web sites for information on exhibits and dates.

➤ Remember: The Champs-Elysees is an ever-evolving, dynamic boulevard filled with culture, history, entertainment, and more. Always check up to the minute sites for the latest information on what's available when.

Chapter 5:

The Louvre: Museum of the Ages

Mona Lisa's cryptic smile, Venus de Milo's glowing torso, the Winged Victory at Samothrace's majestic presence: all of these are housed, along with another 35,000 pieces, within the Musee de Louvre.

Perhaps the most famous museum in the world, the Louvre has earned well-deserved accolades throughout the centuries.

Once the residence of heads of state, this converted palace offers an experience that is unparalleled, containing some of the most famous works of art in all of Western history, as well as antiquities and other objects d'art. The Louvre is truly an education in the contemplation of beauty, from ancient Greece to medieval Europe to nineteenth century France. It is, simply, not to be missed.

Begun at the end of the 12th century, the palace that would become the museum was commissioned by King Phillipe Auguste — it was to be a fortress for kings in an age of crusades and internecine battles. As the city grew up around it, its defensive advantage lessened, and it became more of a palace than a garrison. In the sixteenth century, the Louvre became the royal residence and remained as such, off and on, for the next nearly three hundred years. It was slowly converted into a museum as new offices for government were built following the French Revolution and Napoleonic Wars.

In fact, after the French Revolution, the desire to turn the former palace into a museum was almost immediate. The collection at that time consisted of works that had been in the hands of royalty and the aristocracy.

One of the goals of the revolution was to eradicate the divisions in society brought upon by the stratification of wealth and social class—the end of the monarchy and of the aristocratic system—and thus it was natural that a museum for all the public to enjoy would grow out of the former spoils of the privileged. The Louvre also became a center of learning for both artists and the general public and, amid controversies over renovation and funding, still maintained broad support.

After the world wars, the Louvre underwent major refurbishments and renovations to evolve into the treasure trove that we enjoy to this day. Former French President Francois Mitterand initiated what was called the "Grand Louvre" project in the post-war years, an extensive project that involved turning the previous palace into a museum in its entirety and focusing on creating a welcome and attractive space for visitors from all over the world.

This was the period during which the famous I.M. Pei pyramid was installed; inaugurated in 1989, the pyramid serves as a beacon to draw visitors and locals alike to this remarkable institution. The "Grand Louvre" project was completed circa 1997.

Since then, the Louvre has continued to uphold its primary mission as a curator of great art from ancient times to the nineteenth century, as well as expand its reach via technology and new branches (there is now a Louvre Abu Dhabi, for example). It has also become a true public institution, supported by donors and others, rather than an institution under the auspices of the French government. With its remarkable history and longevity, the Louvre is truly one of the most astonishing places on earth, the largest museum in the world by most accounts, and an incredible, unforgettable experience for any traveler visiting Paris.

The collection of the Louvre is truly staggering; there are roughly 35,000 different objects displayed throughout the sprawling campus, and it would take multiple visits to even begin to take in everything the museum has to offer.

Therefore, the one-time traveler is forced to undertake the task of deciding how must time to spend and where to spend it. While everyone's personal interests vary—and you should peruse the larger Louvre collection for something that meets your personal taste—there are some unforgettable highlights of the Louvre that most experts would agree everyone must see.

The specialties of the museum are in its ancient Greek sculpture collection and its Italian and French painting. Below is a partial list and description of these not to be missed highlights of the greatest museum in the Western world.

Highlights of the Louvre

Ancient Collection

➤ Starting with Greece, you cannot miss out on the renowned Venus de Milo. This sculpture (excepting the missing arms, lost to history) represents everything that classical art stood for: a godlike image of the human form, all proportion and symmetry. Everything is in balance, and this statue reveals the classical preoccupation with the perfection of the human form.

➤ Don't miss the Gallery of Statues, as well, for more takes on classical sculpture. The Greeks often liked to depict forms in motion, so these sculptures show a variety of almost lifelike motion in these ancient works of art. The *contrapposto* poses, which shows the figure resting on one leg, is effective in capturing the fleeting moment before motion begins. While these statues strive for the perfection central to classical art, they also capture something of real life in that near motion posing. These are timeless pieces.

- ➢ There are also stone fragments of the Parthenon to peruse in the Louvre. These pieces came from what was once a temple to Athena at the height of the golden age of Greece. There are gods and goddesses, centaurs and other creatures, humans participating in rituals; the Parthenon Frieze brings ancient Greek culture to life.

- ➢ In addition, there is some Roman statuary in the Louvre, which is interesting to compare to the Greeks. The Romans borrowed much from Greek culture, of course, and their style of sculpture aimed to utilize the Greek notions of perfection but in a more mass-produced form. The best examples of Roman art here are the representations of emperors, particularly Augustus Caesar, which would have been pieces that were produced with more careful thought.

- ➢ The crowning glory of the Louvre's ancient collection is the Winged Victory of Samothrace: she was once the muse at the prow of a ship, long lost to the sea, which was found in the middle of the nineteenth century. She may have lost her head, but she has lost none of her power to command respect and awe. Dated to about 190 BCE, the Winged Victory towers over the ancient collection in all her two tons of carved rock. She is impossible to dismiss.

Medieval and Renaissance Gems

➢ Obviously, the *Mona Lisa* is perhaps the most famous of all the artwork in the Louvre—though one could argue whether that fame is deserved, given the amazing quality of any number of works in the museum. But, yes, the *Mona Lisa* is a must-see, a destination painting. Beware that it hangs behind glass, cordoned off by a rope and that there are always throngs of people waiting to get up close and personal with it. Be patient and work your way slowly through the crowd. It's a surprisingly small painting for having such an outsized reputation; get as close as you can to truly appreciate this da Vinci enigma.

➢ Aside from the Mona Lisa, the Louvre boasts two medieval masterworks that are worth taking a good look at Cimabue's *The Madonna of the Angels* and Giotto's *St. Francis of Assisi Receiving the Stigmata*. Cimabue's work is representative of a lot of the art of medieval Europe; following the fall of Rome in about 500 CE, the world became a chaotic place without much central rule, and these paintings of Mary with Jesus were a comfort to the throngs of believers that lived otherwise short and brutish lives. Giotto's work, on the other hand, is one of great inspiration, and he himself is considered a master of medieval art. This altarpiece is reminiscent of his famed frescoes in the town of Assisi, Italy.

➤ Other Renaissance pieces that warrant a stop are by da Vinci, Raphael, and Veronese. Besides the *Mona Lisa*, the Louvre also displays the da Vinci painting, *Virgin, Child, and St. Anne.* The Anne of the picture bears a striking resemblance to Lisa herself. There are also the da Vinci's *Virgin on the Rocks* and *John the Baptist.* Anyone who has been fascinated by the great painter and inventor should be delighted by the Louvre's collection.

➤ Raphael's work is a refinement of what da Vinci started, and the Louvre houses *La Belle Jardiniere,* one of his best paintings. *La Belle* showcases the familiar Madonna and Child, with John the Baptist alongside, and is the culmination of the Renaissance commitment to the old classical ideals of perfection. There is symmetry and beauty in all of its many brushstrokes.

➤ Finally, the notorious Veronese painting, *The Marriage at Cana,* is a true stunner. This enormous painting fills the room—and the eye—with a thousand minute details and minuscule actions. It is literally teeming with life.

Give it some time, as this painting of the wedding where Jesus turned water into wine has much going on in it and much going for it.

French Favorites

➢ Naturally, a state institution wouldn't be a state institution without some homegrown artists in the collection. The Louvre, of course, is no exception and houses some of the most renowned French painters and paintings of all time. Start with Jacques-Louis David for some serious French pomp and circumstance. His *The Coronation of Napoleon* is a huge propaganda piece lifting the newly crowned emperor to the status of the Roman *ancient regime*. David's neoclassical style is employed on purpose to anoint Napoleon with the same status as, say, Augustus Caesar and the like. It's a big, bold painting for a big, bold legend.

➢ There is also Eugene Delacroix's famous *Liberty Leading the People*. Painted after Napoleon has been exiled, this is another big, bold painting full of ideas. Liberty, in the form of a bare-breasted woman, stands in the center of the frame, waving the French flag and rallying the people of France to stand up for their freedom. The other figures in the painting represent all the various social classes of France, and their drab colors serve to highlight the red, white, and blue of the patriotic flag. As the Musee de Louvre was the first public museum in Europe, this ode to freedom seems fitting.

➤ Another famous painting in this hallway, Theodore Gericault's *The Raft of the Medusa* immortalizes another infamous set of events in history. In contrast to David's neoclassical restraint and grandeur, Gericault's style is that of romanticism, all emotion and turmoil. Based on an actual shipwreck that occurred in the early nineteenth century, this sprawling work cannot but tug at the heart—and serve as a reminder of the perils of travel at that moment in time (not to mention the tragedy of the international slave trade, which is certainly not the focus of the painting but lies underneath).

Practical Considerations

➤ Be sure to get a pass for the Louvre *before* you go: the lines are long enough just to get in. The Paris Pass offers a great deal for travelers spending a few days in

Paris, as it lets you into most major attractions with a minimum of fuss.

> Give yourself at least a couple of hours in the Louvre. Even if you are the most casual observer of art, there will be much to see, some of it utterly central to the history of Western civilization. If you are an art buff, give yourself twice that amount of time.

> Crowds are worst in the mornings and at the beginning of the week, typically speaking.

> There are several cafes sprinkled throughout the museum, all serving fairly good food. Plan a break if you intend to spend more than a couple of hours in the museum.

> Finally, things are always in flux at any museum, much less this enormous one: check in before you travel to find out if anything is closed, under renovation, or to see if there are any special exhibits that you might not want to miss.

Chapter 6:

Montmartre: Bohemian Haven

One of the most charming neighborhoods in Paris, the area of Montmartre is reminiscent of an artist's colony of the late nineteenth and early twentieth centuries, and indeed, served its purpose as such for much of that time.

With cobbled streets and small cafes, Montmartre seems removed from the hustle of the central part of Paris.

It feels like a small community in its own right and boasts some of the most famous landmarks in Paris, from cinema and art history alike.

While Montmartre isn't chock full of monumental sights — its charm is that you can feel like a local while being a tourist — it does claim a couple of sights that most travelers will be thrilled to see.

Set atop a hill in the 18th arrondissement (district), Montmartre was once the center of bohemian artist life in Paris. This is where Toulouse-Lautrec drank absinthe and painted his famous scenes of Paris nightlife (the Moulin Rouge the most famed among them), and he is only one among many artists who once called Montmartre home.

Manet, Renoir, and Van Gogh also haunted the cafes and bars of this mini village, attracted by cheap rents and free-thinking. Montmartre had the whiff of the scandalous about it back in the late nineteenth and early twentieth centuries; this is where you could catch a glimpse of young ladies' underwear during the notorious cancan shows at the Moulin Rouge and other, less infamous nightclubs.

It was (and is) also renowned for its lovely landscape—the greenest part of Paris—which was another inevitable draw for artists. It also didn't hurt that liquor was untaxed in this part of the city. It became a draw for artists, dreamers, and poets alike. Its importance to the history of twentieth-century art cannot be understated: for one example among many, Picasso painted his hugely important and impressive *Les Mademoiselles d'Avignon* in the area. If you wander the neighborhood, you will see commemorative plaques adorning the houses where many famous artists once lived.

You can also still find numerous eclectic galleries throughout the district and don't miss the Montmartre Museum, which pays homage to the many artists who have lived in this area. It features recreations of the whole cabaret scene that first made this district famous (or notorious, depending on your point of view) and resides in the former mansion of Renoir. The original posters alone are worth a trip. There is also a small museum devoted solely to the works of Salvador Dali, the famous Spanish surrealist. Below is a partial list of the highlights that can be seen on your visit to Montmartre.

> ➤ The heart of this village within a city is the place du Tertre, which is still lined with cafes and restaurants, bars and other emporiums. This is where the original

bohemians spent time, drinking and thinking and sharing ideas. It can be quite crowded on weekends, especially when the weather is nice, but this is all part of the fun, really. Its reputation as the most artsy district in Paris still yet holds true in the place du Tertre, where artists and cartoonists set up easels each day—both to amuse the tourists and to make a living. Here you can find a truly original, non-mass-produced souvenir to take home with you, another perk of the trip.

> Montmartre also lays claim to many restaurants, romantic and otherwise, where you can enjoy gourmet food and relax. The street is lined with cafes, with the tables facing outward so that you can people watch to your heart's content. Some of the more renowned establishments are the Café des Deux Moulins, the Au Rendez-Vous des Amis, and Chamarre, a high-end restaurant at the top of the hill. There is also a restaurant atop the roof of the Terrass Hotel which provides stunning views, especially at night.

> Of course, if you happen to be in Montmartre at night, there is no shortage of entertainment options: first and foremost, the famed Moulin Rouge is located here, still operating nightly shows for hordes of tourists. If you are an enormous fan of *Belle Epoque*-era Paris, then by all means, the show might just be for you; it is

expensive and touristy, but still a lot of fun. Be aware that the area in which the infamous windmill is positioned is a bit dicey: there are sex shops and rowdy bars all around. In addition to the Moulin Rouge are the Au Lapin Agile, which also hosts a cabaret, and the Moulin de la Galette, the dance hall featured in Renoir's famous *Dance at the Moulin de Galette.* You can soak up a little history along with your drink in Montmartre.

➢ In terms of sights, the Sacre-Coeur Basilica is the most striking in Montmartre. This cathedral offers the absolute best view of Paris, short of climbing the Eiffel Tower, even from ground level. If you climb to the top of the dome—the stairs are rather claustrophobic but it's only about 300 steps—then you witness a panorama of the city that rivals even the view from the tower. Inside the basilica, the largest mosaic in France resides, showing an ebullient Jesus with his heart burning with unending love for all humankind (hence, "Sacred Heart" Basilica). While the church looks ancient, with its bleached white glow, it was built only about a hundred years ago. Its position at the top of Paris's highest hill gives it a special splendor.

➢ Beyond these famous landmarks, there are other things to do and see in Montmartre. For one, the deepest Metro station in Paris happens to take you directly to Montmartre: take the Metro to Abessess to plunge deep into the underbelly of Paris. You can also shop along the Rue de Steinkerque, which hosts a number of little shops selling t-shirts and trinkets—this area is rife for bargaining and for finding a kitschy souvenir (it can also be rife for pickpockets and the like, so do be cautious). On Saturday morning, this little street is particularly busy. It also boasts a number of cafes that you can stop and have a rest and a snack, such as La Cure Gourmande and Maison George Larnicol Chocolaterie. This area is in direct opposition to the glitz and glamor of the Champs-Elysees; this is the place to find a bargain.

➢ You can also visit the Bateau-Lavoir, which is a mini-park located in what used to be a piano factory. This is the location where all the bohemian artists would gather in order to save money on heat while exchanging ideas and banter. Picasso once said of it, "I know we will make it through in the Bateau Lavoir. There we were truly happy; we were considered as painters and not as curious animals." This was a place where kindred spirits and original minds sought refuge.

➢ There are also a couple of minor museums in the area, the Musee de la Vie Romantique, dedicated to all things romantic in art, and the Musee d'Art Naif Max Fourny, dedicated to the *brut* art of Fourny among others. The Romantique is a former residence turned salon where many artists used to work and now offers special exhibits and events, as well as a small permanent offering of works by artists such as George Sand, Eugene Delacroix, and the musicians Frederic Chopin and Franz Liszt. The Max Fourny museum celebrates the *brut* (or raw) art of its namesake, with over 500 paintings and 80 sculptures. The *art brut* movement champions work of untrained artists and found methods, rather than strenuously trained creation. There is also, for the not-so-faint at heart, the Musee de l'Erotisme which is certainly not for young children. Enter at your own desire.

In short, Montmartre is a bustling bohemian district with a fascinating artistic past and a fun, invigorating present. Spend a day here, touring the Sacre-Coeur Basilica and walking the streets that once were crowded with some of the most famous artists of the day, stopping in at a café or two and doing a bit of shopping. End your trip with a show at the notorious Moulin Rouge or a drink at one of the fabulous bars — you might just get inspired to create your own renowned art!

Chapter 7:

Le Marais: Fashion Forward

Another must-see neighborhood in Paris, Le Marais has become perhaps the trendiest part of the entire city. While its name technically translates as "the swamp," today's Marais is anything but: filled with fashion boutiques, hip nightclubs, and LGBTQ friendly haunts, Le Marais is one of the most atmospheric sections of the city.

Located in the 3rd and 4th arrondissements, on the right bank of the Seine River, the neighborhood is slightly less touristy than other areas of Paris, catering to upwardly mobile young professionals and other denizens of the fashion scene. This part of Paris is not to be missed, from its shops and entertainment to its sites and culture.

Starting in the 17th century, the former swamp land of the Le Marais area began to take shape as one the fashionable places in the City of Lights: aristocrats began to build private mansions there, close to the fashionable Place des Vosges and near one of the king's townhouses. It became a place for the rich and powerful to gather and to gossip — and to escape the increasingly crowded (and sometimes polluted) central part of Paris. After the French Revolution dismantled the aristocracy, Le Marais became a working-class neighborhood, home to various artists and central to Paris's immigrant community, particularly the Jewish community. Le Marais still boasts old cobblestone streets and pre-Revolution spirit; while much of Paris was razed in the 1800s and rebuilt, Le Marais was spared this reconstruction. Thus, it retains much of its *ancient regime* charm.

Le Marais was also home to the infamous Bastille prison, in which the Marquis de Sade wrote his rather shocking treatises and at which the French Revolution truly got underway — but don't bother looking for it. It was eventually torn day and all that is left is the plaza in which it once stood. Nevertheless, it remains a historic place where the ideas of liberte, egalite, and fraternite (liberty, equality, and brotherhood) rocked French society and culture, reverberating through to the present day.

There are numerous things to do and to see in Le Marais, and the best way to explore all of it is to give yourself a few hours to stroll through the neighborhood, taking in the sites and relaxing at one (or two) or the charming cafes along the way. Stay until nighttime to enjoy the entertaining and usually relaxed nightlife that the area has to offer. Below is a partial list of the best of what Le Marais has to offer.

> Don't miss the Place de Vosges which has been fashionable since the 17th century. At one point in time, it was Paris's most exclusive neighborhood, and you can still see the old mansions lining each side of the street. They were built around Henry IV's palace, so that aristocrats could have ready access to the king. A statue of Henry's son, Louis XIII, sits in the middle of the plaza, surrounded by the old mansions, new cafes, and small art galleries.

- Be sure to check out the most famous of the ancient residences, the Hotel de Sully, built in the early part of the 17th century. One of the grandest of the old mansions, the Hotel de Sully now houses a small souvenir shop and some lovely gardens through which you can walk. Today, the preservation of historic sites and landmarks is managed within this building.

- Another of the *hotels* worth a look is the Hotel de Ville de Paris, which doesn't allow interior access but has a beautiful neo-classical exterior and grounds that turn into an ice-skating rink in winter, boasts a beautiful display of magnolia blossoms in spring, and hosts concerts frequently in summer. To get a look from above, go across the street to Le Perchoir Marais where you can have a cocktail and an excellent view.

- You can also visit La Maison de Victor Hugo, the internationally famous author of *Les Miserables* and *The Hunchback of Notre Dame*. Before he was exiled for his unstinting support for Napoleon I, Hugo lived and wrote here. Entrance to this small museum is free, with paintings and memorabilia of the family. It also houses temporary exhibits at various times (some of these have admission fees but viewing them is optional).

- Just about every neighborhood of note in Paris has a stunning church, from Notre Dame to Le Sacre-Coeur, and Marais is no exception. The charming Eglise Saint Paul Saint Louis was also built during Le Marais' original heyday in the 17th century, and during the Revolution briefly became a refuge for some radical Enlightenment thinkers who called themselves the Cult of Reason. After the Revolution, at the beginning of the 19th century, it was returned to its function as a Catholic house of worship.

➢ You also don't want to miss the Rue des Rosiers, or the Jewish Quarter. This was once the largest enclave of Jewish dwellers in Western Europe, and it still retains its distinctive cultural feel. Along this street are kosher restaurants and lots of fast casual places selling Mediterranean specialties such as falafel, shawarma, and kefta. You can also still find a number of excellent delis specializing in various Jewish delicacies, from babkas and challah to gefilte fish and piroshkis (dumplings). There are also some small art galleries along the Rue displaying Jewish-themed art, and if you are interested in spending some time here, there are always community events that celebrate various aspects of Jewish history and culture throughout the year. Be aware that most of the shops close on the Jewish Sabbath, which is Saturday.

➢ On the nearby Rue de Temple, there is also a Jewish Art and History Museum which tells the story of the Jewish presence in Europe. It is an immersive educational experience—here's where you can learn about bar mitzvahs and menorahs—with traditional objects, costumes, and artwork.

➤ If you're interested in art, then look no further than the stunning Pompidou Center: this striking building, with its primary colors and exposed exterior pipes and escalator, houses some of the greatest Modern art found in the world. Not only does the museum have some Modern greats—Picasso, Matisse, Dali, Kandinsky—but it also houses lesser-known artists from the post-war period up through the 1960s, as well as constantly rotating special exhibits. Outside the museum, there are always street performers working and oftentimes outdoor concerts in nicer weather. The view from the rooftop is also worth a trek.

➤ Another of the old mansions in Le Marais has been converted into the Picasso Museum, which as its name suggests, is a shrine to perhaps the greatest artist of the 20th century, Pablo Picasso. More than 5000 of his works, from paintings and sculptures to drawings and manuscripts: this is a must-see for any devotee of the great man.

➤ If you like museums of history, visit the Carnavalet Museum, which showcases French history from the time of the Sun King, Louis XIV, to the *Belle-Epoque.*

Perhaps the biggest draw in this museum is its excellent section covering the most torturous, bloody, and ultimately culture-altering period in French history: The Revolution. From the Bastille to the guillotine, this display is rightfully lauded, with portraits of all the major players in the Revolution—including the man who would ultimately betray the ideals of it, Napoleon.

➤ For another slice of history in Le Marais, you can visit the sprawling Pere Lachaise Cemetery: this quasi-park is wonderful for a casual stroll, and you can find the grave sites of numerous luminaries from French history, such as Chopin, Moliere, and Edith Piaf. You can even find the markers for the ill-fated lovers of medieval poetry, Heloise and Abelard. This is also where you will find the grave sites of English writer Oscar Wilde, who lived his last days here in self-imposed exile, and Jim Morrison, the self-destructive lead singer of The Doors. While it used to be a pilgrimage to visit Morrison's grave to leave a tribute or a scrawl upon his headstone, in recent years, this has been better policed and frowned upon.

➤ Besides all of the sites and museums of note, Le Marais is a fun place to do some shopping: for antiques and other vintage souvenirs, try the shops at Village St-Paul; for a unique Le Marais experience, travel the Passage de L'Ancre, one of the oldest streets in Paris, where you can find a quaint umbrella repair shop amidst the residential housing; or for the ultimate French-style department store experience, check out Le BHV, which sells everything from housing goods to vintage clothing to food and beyond. Le BHV also has a Starbucks inside, as well as some small restaurant options.

> Finally, don't miss all of the food experiences that can be had in Le Marais: from the ubiquitous cafes (try The Broken Arm for a high concept experience) to the sweet shops (try Carette for macarons). Don't miss out on all the international offerings here, as well, particularly in the Jewish Quarter (try L'As Du Fallafel for some of the best).

Chapter 8:

The Islands: Ile de la Cité and Beyond

Many people are unaware that Paris owes its very existence to the presence of the mighty Seine River — which was once used as a means for strategic defense and as a shipping network — and that Paris itself is a city of islands. This strategy of establishing towns and cities near great waterways was employed all over Europe in the medieval period and before (London has the Thames; Venice has its lagoon and canals).

The Seine River flows far beyond Paris, of course, from Burgundy to Normandy, it is in Paris where its romantic and cultural power reach their apotheosis. While there are more than the four islands discussed below in Paris proper, these four islands are filled with all of the things that make the city a wonderful, exciting, and historic place to visit. Without the Seine and its islands, Paris would likely never have become the capital of one of the most powerful states in Western Europe.

At nearly 800 kilometers in length, the Seine is a long and winding river that runs through the heart of France. The stretch that runs through the City of Lights is called the Traversée de Paris and hosts several small islands, with four main ones laying claim to any number of museums and monuments, churches and historic streets, restaurants and entertainment, and more. Below are listed the four main *Iles* of Paris with a guide to what's available to explore on each.

Ile de la Cité: Heart of a City

This small island is literally where Paris got its start via the internationally renowned — and now tragically damaged — Notre Dame Cathedral. The Ile da la Cite ("Island of the City") is where you will find the oldest sites in Paris, as well as bustling cafes and mercantilism. It is truly the center of Paris, and a traveler could easily spend an entire day here exploring this largest of the Paris's islands. Following is a list of the attractions on Ile de la Cite, including some institutions that reside on the Left Bank — technically not on the island itself but such a part of Paris's artistic heritage as to be merged with it.

> ➤ Entire books have been written about the grand lady of France, Notre Dame: it occupies the literal center of France itself, the point from which all distances were measured. The symbol of Paris since medieval times, Notre Dame surpasses even the Eiffel Tower for many as the enduring representation of what it means to be Parisian. It was begun in 1163 by people so pious and devoted that they gave labor and materials for free, with no hope of ever seeing this mighty cathedral completed during their lifetimes. Indeed, the first Mass held in Notre Dame did not take place until nearly two

centuries later, in 1345. Originally the site of a Roman temple dedicated to Jupiter, Notre Dame stands on what every conquering tribe felt was a sacred location. Famous for its gothic architecture—those flying buttresses—and its gloomy gargoyles, Notre Dame is beautiful inside and out. Besides those oft-noted details, the façade of Notre Dame depicts a number of religious tales, the most notable being that of Saint Denis who was beheaded but kept going until he found consecrated ground to meet the Lord. This is on the left door when you face the entryway. On the central door is the story of the Last Judgment, and above the doorways are statues of the Kings of Judah. Within the cathedral, you will walk the long central nave up to the altar, with its beautiful pieta (a pieta is a depiction of Mary holding the body of Christ). In the right transept, there is a stature of Joan of Arc, a patron saint of sorts in France. In this area is also a famed stained-glass window, which still contains the original medieval glass (at least prior to the fire). There are also several small chapels surrounding the central nave, each dedicated to a different saint. Filled with light, this gothic structure revels in its spires ascending toward the heavens, all to be closer to god. It is not to be missed, even in its damaged state.

- Lest we forget, Notre Dame is not the only soaring gothic cathedral on the Ile da la Cite: there is also that pinnacle of stained glass, Saint-Chapelle. Begun almost a century after Our Lady, Saint-Chapelle was—however unlikely seeming—completed within only six years, from 1242 until 1248. This speedy construction contributes to its sense of architectural harmony; there weren't two centuries of different rulers and differing opinions on how to put it up. Essentially, Saint-Chapelle was erected in order to showcase stained glass; thus, the exterior is not as elaborate or beautiful as Notre Dame, but the interior is a triumph of light and art. There are depictions of various biblical stories in the glass, including Judgment Day in the famous Rose Window. The altar itself looms high above the nave, as it was built to showcase the alleged actual Crown of Thorns. Saint-Chapelle is most definitely worth a visit, especially if access to Notre Dame is blocked.
- Just outside Saint-Chapelle, across the Boulevard du Palais is one of the few survivors of the original signs for the Paris subway, typically called the Metro. This Art Nouveau landmark, with its "Metropolitan" signage, is considered a national treasure.
- Also, near Saint-Chapelle is the potentially gloomy Concierge, the prison in which people were held before they were marched to the guillotine during the years of

the Revolution and beyond. It held 2,780 citizens who were finally executed, including the notorious Marie Antoinette. You can walk through this well-preserved landmark to see a memorial to those who were killed at the site, as well as a recreation of Marie Antoinette's very cell. A turning point in France's history, the Concierge marks the darkest part of the French Revolution.

➢ At the other end of the Ile de la Cite, you will find the Deportation Memorial, dedicated to the French victims of the Nazi concentration camps and occupation. About 200,000 French citizens died during the occupation of France, and this memorial honors them with 200,000 lighted crystals. It is a light-filled tribute to those who were unjustly murdered. The message, as at many other Holocaust sites, is placed above the exit: "Forgive, but never forget."

➢ Sites along the Left Bank near the Ile de la Cite include the many booksellers who have set up shop here since medieval times, and the brick-and-mortar Shakespeare & Co bookstore, so important to early 20th century literary history. It is also the most preserved part of medieval Paris, largely escaping the mania for public planning that engulfed the city in the nineteenth century. There is also another church of note, St. Severin, which allows you to examine the infamous gothic gargoyles up close. And, at the Place St. Michel, you stand at the center of Paris's famous bohemian scene, where poets and artists, philosophers and drinkers held court for many years. This is in the famed Latin Quarter, about which the following chapter will delve into detail.

Ile Saint-Louis: Sweet Sibling

Considered the sister island to the Ile de la Cite, this island is home to lots of shops and cafes. It also largely escaped renovation and thus retains some of its cobblestone streets and medieval charm. It wasn't developed until the 17th century, when it was intended as a retreat for the wealthiest of Parisians, including King Louis XIII. It still remains one of the priciest, poshest places in Paris to set up a residence. While there aren't a lot of sites of historic note on this island, there are lots of boutique shops, high-end restaurants, and cozy art galleries. In particular, Ile Saint-Louis is noted for its fabulous sweet shops, including the Paris institution, Berthillon. It also hosts the Pont Marie, an alleged lover's bridge where one should kiss one's companion for luck and longevity.

Ile Aux Cygnes: Outdoor Art

While this small island is off the beaten path for most tourists, it does lay claim to some interesting outdoor art. The most famous monument is the replica of the Statue of Liberty which stands 22 meters high at the southernmost point of the island. It was given to France in 1889 by American citizens of French descent to commemorate the hundred-year anniversary of the French Revolution. Another famous statue on the island is the *La France Renaissante*, which was given to France by the Danish community in 1930; it celebrates the revival of French culture that marked the beginning of the twentieth century. Finally, you can also visit the Pont de Bir-Hakeim, an early twentieth-century bridge that features stone reliefs depicting Science, Labor, Electricity, and Commerce. It was renamed after a 1942 battle between France and Germany.

Ile Louviers: Small and Charming

The smallest of the four islands, and by far the most off the beaten path, Ile Louviers feels like a village in and of itself. You can come here to marvel at the architecture, do some shopping—it's a particularly good place for books—and sit at a café, enjoying the weather and the people. Ile Louviers, technically, is no longer an actual island as the tiny stretch of water that separated it from the mainland was filled in during the nineteenth century. Still, this is the kind of place that, if you are a tourist looking to slow down and smell the coffee, is perfect for a quiet day.

Chapter 9:

Latin Quarter: Melting Pot of Paris

Located on the Left Bank, the Latin Quarter was long the center of French artistic and intellectual life. It is also home to large immigrant communities, thus fueling a bohemian atmosphere and a cultural diaspora that gives rise to good food and interesting exchanges.

People from all over Europe were once drawn to this area because of the University of Paris, founded in 1215—hence, "Latin" Quarter, as Latin was the lingua franca of scholars and religious leaders throughout the middle ages. Today, many of the immigrants are of Greek descent—you will find many gyro shops—or from the Middle East. But its multiethnic feel is nothing new: the Latin Quarter has been the melting pot of Paris for at least the last 800 years.

Its narrow and tangled alleyways represent an older Paris, before city planning razed much of this confusing cobblestone structure. It's the perfect counterpart to a day spent roaming the Ile de la Cite, with all its massive monuments and historic touchstones. The Latin Quarter is for fun, food, and atmosphere—lively and eclectic, both touristy and authentic. Below is a partial list of what you can see and do in this notable neighborhood; you could devote about half a day here without running out of fun and interesting things to encounter.

> ➤ Across the Seine from Notre Dame cathedral resides the Saint-Michel Fountain, a good place to begin your journey through the Latin Quarter. Commissioned in the nineteenth century during Paris's extensive renovations, this fountain is not nearly as old as much

of what you might encounter in the neighborhood. While it was controversial at the beginning of its commission, it has become a favorite gathering place for locals and a destination spot for tourists. Many different sculptors contributed to the fountain, which accounts for its diversity of styles—which some see as a negative, others as a positive. It concerns the battle between good and evil, represented by Saint Michel's duel with, and ultimate victory over, the devil.

➢ Near the fountain is the historic Rue de la Huchette, dating back about 800 years. Lined with lots of (very touristy) restaurants, this street also has some legitimate sites, in particular the La Theatre de la Huchette. This small theater has been putting on the same Ionesco plays—*The Lesson* and *The Bald Soprano*—for over 50 years. Talk about dedication. The street also hosts one of the oldest jazz clubs in all of Paris, Le Caveau de la Huchette, where you can take in an evening of entertainment. This is also the area in which you will find Shakespeare & Co., the famous bookstore founded by Sylvia Beach and frequented by the famous expatriate American writers of the early twentieth century, including Hemingway and Gertrude Stein. Beach was also justifiably famous for publishing

James Joyce's masterwork, *Ulysses*, at a time when nobody else would because of its supposed obscenity.

➢ You can also visit the Museum of the Middle Ages which resides in the Latin Quarter. The museum complex was built around the much older Roman relic, the Lutetia thermal baths. It also houses one of the most famous tapestry displays of the Middle Ages, *The Lady and the* Unicorn, a sequence of six well-preserved hangings. Under renovation until the end of 2020, parts of the museum are still open to visitors, including part of the Roman baths and the section housing *The Lady and the Unicorn.*

➢ The Latin Quarter is also where the University of Paris was founded, and perhaps the most famous institution that still indicates sophistication in art and education is the Sorbonne. Originally a college of the University of Paris, today the Sorbonne is its own institution, encompassing a number of various colleges itself. Its grand dome stands high above the area, recognizable to any visiting scholar. If you have the time, you can visit the lovely Sainte Genevieve Library, which houses a number of medieval manuscripts and other historical objects of note.

➢ While most people are familiar with the famous Pantheon in Rome, many do not know that there is also a Pantheon in Paris: it was built in the eighteenth century as a tribute to Sainte Genevieve, the patron saint of Paris, on the site where she was allegedly buried after being killed by invading Huns trying to protect the city. Over time, the Pantheon was transformed into a mausoleum for French citizens of note are buried. You can find the final resting places of Voltaire, Rousseau, Victor Hugo, Alexander Dumas, and Marie Curie, among others. In addition, it houses the original Foucault's Pendulum, which demonstrates—without electronic power—the earth's rotation. It is also architecturally interesting in its own right, with its neo-classical design.

➤ About the time you start to feel puckish, think about gathering the materials for a picnic in the lovely Luxembourg gardens. Located near the Palace of Luxembourg (which is not open to the public), the gardens boast a number of fountains and pools, with a serene outdoor atmosphere that is best enjoyed in the late spring and early fall. The Medici Fountain is perhaps the best known of the structures in the park, and there is also a marvelous kitchen garden and a beehive center.

➤ You might try the Rue Mouffetard for your picnic victuals: the street is home to a number of restaurants and bars, as well as street markets and vendors. If you don't venture there to get picnic supplies or stop in there for a leisurely bite at a café, you might be tempted to return at night, when the atmosphere is perhaps the most convivial in all of Paris. It can even be a little bit rowdy in this usually most etiquette-conscious of cities. This is a hub for young people looking for a fun and interesting time.

➢ In addition to the aforementioned Roman baths within the Museum of the Middle Ages, there are some free-standing Roman ruins that you can find within the Latin Quarter. Across from the Rue Monge are the remains of a Roman amphitheater, known as the Lutetia arenas. Visible there are some of the circular seating which would allow spectators to view theater (and gladiators, though this small amphitheater was probably intended more for plays and the like), as well as a raised stage on which actors and other would perform. While small and less notable than the Roman ruins you will find in southern France, this gives you a quick glimpse into the ancient world and is worth a look if you won't be traveling to Arles or Nimes.

➢ As mentioned in the introduction, the Latin Quarter is now home to a sizable Arab and Muslim population, as well, and there are some landmarks that recognize and honor this. There is the Institut du Monde Arabe (Arab World Institute), which aims to educate visitors about the vast and diverse Arab culture across the globe.

There is also the beautiful Great Paris Mosque, which was built following World War I, using architectural and design techniques similar to the much older Spanish-Moorish buildings (which harken from the medieval period). It isn't open to the public on Fridays—the Muslim holy day—but on other days, you can take a tour of the mosque and its gardens and enjoy tea and pastries, if you like. This is a site that is not on most tourist's lists, but it is quite a grand experience if you have the time.

➢ The Latin Quarter also lays claim to a botanical garden, the Jardin des Plantes, which has the most comprehensive selection of plants in all of France currently. This is a great place to explore for educational purposes, as well as a relaxing place just to stroll and enjoy the beauty and weather.

➢ Finally, this area also contains the Paris's Natural History Museum, where you can enjoy exhibits in paleontology and mineralogy among other natural phenomena. Perhaps its biggest draw is its Gallery of Evolution which shows the long biological history of the planet.

Whether you spend half a day here or visit in the evening for some good food and raucous entertainment, the Latin Quarter shouldn't be missed.

With its medieval feel and proximity to the great monuments of the Ile de la Cite, it showcases an intoxicating mix of cultural diversity and historic importance.

Chapter 10:

Beyond the Centre: Looking for the Unusual and Unexplored

Certainly, Paris has all of the blockbusters to offer—the Eiffel Tower, the Louvre, Notre Dame, and so on—but it also a whole host of other things to see and do that aren't as well known. From smaller museums to interesting activities, some of the ideas here are fairly well-known to many while other ideas here are truly off the beaten path.

Thus, if you have a particular interest in a particular pastime or hobby or activity, or if you are lucky enough to spend more than a few days in Paris, then here is a guide for some out of the ordinary sites and activities that any visitor can engage in. These are the kinds of things that might just make you feel more like a native than a tourist.

- ➤ If you enjoy exploring museums, there are many lesser-known—and typically quirky—museums sprinkled throughout Paris, some of which have been mentioned in previous chapters and some of which will be mentioned throughout this list. Start with the Musee d'Ennery and its amazing collection of Asian art. Housed in the former mansion of Clemence d'Ennery, the more than 7000 pieces in the museum contain porcelains, ivories, sculptures, furniture, and some marvelous trunks inlaid with elaborate carvings and ornamentation. It is truly a hidden gem, but do plan if you decide to go, as it accommodates small groups for only two Saturdays per month.

- ➤ One of the most foolproof ways to start feeling as Parisian as possible is to attend a Paris Salon, or trade show. There are several throughout the year, so do your research on dates before you book your trip, or before you go, to see if there are any during your stay. For one example, there is the venerable Salon des Vins et

Vignerons Independants which brings together about 500 winemakers from all over France; for the price of a ticket, you get a tasting glass and access to a whole world of French wine, as well as some gourmet nibbles to keep you fortified. There is also the Salon de Chocolat, which as you can guess, is a trade show featuring all things chocolate. Usually held in the fall, this fun event even features a fashion show—with models wearing chocolate. Or, you can time your event to coincide with the nine-day extravaganza that is the Salon International d'Agriculture, which showcases food and agricultural products (and livestock) from all over France and around the world. This is like a state fair in the Midwest, but with the flair and sophistication that you can find nowhere else quite like you can in Paris.

➤ If you're seeking out a little exercise and really want to go deep with the locals, take a swim in one of Paris's amazing pools. The Piscine Pontoise is illuminated from below, allowing swimmers to bask in the warm glow all the way up until midnight. It's also fairly conveniently located for the tourist, as it is situated between Notre Dame and the Jardin des Plantes. Another option for swimming is at Butte-aux-Cailles, with its three indoor-outdoor pools, all fed by a natural spring. There is also the interesting opportunity to swim atop the Seine

River—one really wouldn't want to swim in it—on the Piscine Josephine Baker which floats along the river with sunbathers and swimmers alike.

> If you're more into relaxation than exertion, then you could seek out one of the rooftop bars sprinkled throughout Paris and enjoy a cocktail with a view. A luxurious (read: expensive) option would be to frequent the L'Oiseau Blanc atop the Peninsula Hotel. Named for a plane that disappeared back in 1927, the bar keeps a replica of its namesake suspended outside. A rather less expensive option, but still no less impressive in the view, is the 43 Up the Roof Bar which sits atop the Holiday Inn Notre Dame. Open at 5:00 pm each day, the bar offers stunning, panoramic views of the entire city.

> But, before you go out drinking or after you've had your cocktail, make sure to get into the contemporary French food scene. There are a couple of places where you can really make like a local and experience the best of French food. Head out to the Rue de Nil in the second arrondissement near the Montmartre neighborhood. This is where a new food empire has been launched by lauded chef Gregory Marchand: Frenchie is the flagship of the group (with reservations nigh impossible to get), while Frenchie's Bar a Vins allows a traveler—who may just drop in—a taste of why Marchand's food is so

popular. There is even a Frenchie to Go, a fast-casual option at the low end of the empire. Also, along this street is a stop for the ultimate coffee break, L'Arbre a Café, which uses only single-source beans from unusual places. If you are looking to supply yourself for a picnic, stop in at Terroirs d'Avenir has cheese, meats, and other charcuterie, as well as top-flight produce, to set you up in style.

➤ Another foodie destination is the Rue Cler, where grocery shopping and dining take center stage. The outdoor market wares contain the best produce from the famous Les Halles market, while wine shops, fromageries (cheese shops), poisonneries (fish shops), charcuteries (meat shops), and boulangeries (bread shops) line the street. There is also a spice market, a chocolate shop, a store specializing in olive products (such as the finest extra virgin olive oil that France produces), and a place to get a good cigar. In addition to all of the places where you can find souvenirs—read up on guidelines to know what you can bring back with you in Chapter 13—and picnic supplies, there are also a number of small cafes where you can get a wonderful meal.

➤ If you'd like to try something truly unique on the food front, why not dine with an actual Parisian in an actual Parisian home? The new VizEat allows visitors to explore a range of options, from a family-style dinner to a romantic dinner for two, to dine with a Parisian resident. It includes menus for you to peruse, as well, and locations that are best suited to your needs. Talk about diving into the Parisian scene!

➢ If you need a break from all the walking you've been doing (or, alas, if the weather turns inclement), then consider taking in a bit of cinema. One of the best places to do this at the Luxour theater, which is a designated historical monument and an excellent place to take in an artsy film. Its Art Deco façade, done up in faux-Egyptian style, is unmistakable, and the theater shows a lot of American films and has a café-bar with a terrace and views of the Sacre-Coeur. Another interesting theater is La Pagode, which is an actual pagoda brought in from Japan and restored as a theater, where it shows international, artsy films; it also has a garden in which you can have a restorative tea. There is also the Rex Grand, a Baroque-inspired theater dating from 1932, which boasts the largest screening room in all of Europe. Finally, you might not want to miss out on the relatively new Foundation Pathe, which houses a movie museum as well as a small theater, with sculptures of Rodin in the lobby.

➢ Once you've savored some 20th century art and 21st century technology, get back to exploring cultural themes by checking out some other small museums: the Musee Zadkine, near the Luxembourg Gardens, is a lovely little museum with a magnificent sculpture garden. The husband and wife artists, sculptor Ossip Zadkine and painter Valentine Prax, left this museum for all to enjoy. Don't miss out on the Musee de la vie Romantique, either, with its tea salon out in the garden, open mid-March through mid-October. And don't forget about Musee Rodin, near the Eiffel Tower, which showcases all things Rodin.

> If you really want to get interactive with activities in Paris, there are several workshops offered in various fields at various places. The Luxembourg Gardens offers a workshop in photography, while the Louvre offers various workshops for kids and adults alike on art. There are also classes for visitors to immerse themselves in French and all things French at the Musse d'Orsay, Les Arts Decoratifs, and 104 Centquatre (that is, little English is spoken in workshops). You can even sign up for a quick workshop that allows you to create a tote bag that will commemorate your time in France; this is offered by the American artist, Kasia Detz.

> If you prefer to consume your art rather than make it, and if you happen to have a sweet tooth, run, don't walk, to renowned Saint-Germain-des-Pres which is

home to several outstanding chocolatiers all within a few blocks. Patrick Roger's shop is home to amazing chocolate sculptures; he even did one of a Rodin for the museum's re-opening after renovation. You can also find the wares of Jean-Charles Rouchoux, another artist working in the medium of chocolate. There are also the shops of Henri Le Roux, who allegedly created the salted caramel chocolate, and Pierre Herme, the legendary pastry chef. The French institution, Maison du Chocolat, is also located in this area. Not only is this a great place to indulge, the Saint-Germain-des-Pres is also an excellent place to pick up some memorable souvenirs.

➢ If you're headed out to the Gare de Lyon train station anyway, be sure to check out the brasserie that's tucked away in the station: after a renovation in 2013, this Belle Epoque classic serves excellent food in an eye-popping setting. Surrounded by 19th century murals and portraits of Parisians, you can enjoy a meal in high style before your trip, or you can grab a prepared meal to take with you on the train, if you like.

➢ Don't miss out on Paris's market scene, as well; these street markets capture the quintessential experience of Parisian daily life. Try the Rue des Martyrs, which has everything from jewelry shops and antique stores to gourmet food vendors and coffee bars. There is also the

Rue Montorgueil which specializes in the finest of fine French foods and gourmet supplies, from oysters and cheese to wine and pastries. It also boasts one of the best cooking supply stores in all of France, E. Dehillerin, where Julia Child herself used to shop. There is also the Rue Mouffetard where every day is market day, with gorgeous produce, dozens of vendors, and plenty of cafes to occupy your time.

➤ If you are really into the food scene, you might also want to set aside some of your time taking part in a cooking class. There are literally dozens to choose from in Paris, from small, intimate lessons in someone's home to large groups taking tours of markets and learning to cook with ingredients. There's something for just about anyone who'd like to participate in such a class—way more interesting than a t-shirt as a souvenir. Try Le Foodist, for one, or the pricier but amazing Ecole de Cuisine Alain Ducasse, a name that signifies the very best.

➤ Another quintessentially local activity that any tourist in the know can take part in is one of the many *bal populaire*'s that are held throughout the city. These public balls are part of a long tradition derived from working class celebrations of various holidays and other causes for celebration, usually involving lots of wine and food along with the dance. These kinds of parties crop up all over France around Bastille Day, with city halls and other locales hosting *bal des pompiers* (or, firemen's balls), where you might even get to see a faux strip tease from some of the firemen themselves. Once a month, the 104 Centquatre, a contemporary arts center in Paris, they throw a *bal populaire* with themes that change each month. These free events are listed on the center's web site, so you can find out dates and themes before you go.

➢ If you start to feel stymied by the hustle and bustle of the city, or if you just enjoy nature, you could check out the Le Petite Ceinture (The Little Belt): this is a 19-mile stretch of abandoned railways that rings the entire city, and for more than a decade now, a new section has been opened up for hiking and exploration. While there are potential plans in place to develop certain sectors of this area, the debates rage on as to what to do with them. For now, you can enjoy the vast range of biodiversity that exists just outside the city limits and spend a beautiful day out in nature, just mere meters away from one of the most industrialized cities on earth. The sections near the 12th, 13th, and 16th arrondissements are said to be the best for enjoyment.

➢ If you enjoy nature but don't necessarily want to be out in it yourself, check out the small but fascinating Musee de la Chasse et de la Nature in the Hotel Guenegard.

This museum is a tribute to all things hunting related, which may sound less interesting than it actually is: here you will find nature paintings alongside antique weapons and animal taxidermy, as well as drawers full of discoveries, such as animal scat. There are also multimedia presentations and nocturnal tours on Thursdays that focus on different natural activities that you can engage in within the city. The museum is also dedicated to conservation causes.

➤ While most of the best cathedrals and basilicas in Paris have already been mentioned, here is the place to note that many of them conduct regular concerts that are free and open to the public. Whether you are a believer or not, these concerts are beautiful expressions of devotion in ancient spaces with excellent acoustics. Check out the web sites of individual churches or Paris tourism sites to find out when and where one of these might be taking place during your visit.

➤ Discover a relatively unknown neighborhood, Mouzaia, or the Quartier d'Amerique. Built over abandoned quarries, the neighborhood's cottages date from the late nineteenth and early twentieth century and are now home to writers, artists, and celebrities. There are also nice restaurants, some cafes, and nightlife to be found in the area.

> Finally, there is always something waiting just to be discovered in Paris: keep your eyes open, your ears tuned in, and your senses on high alert, and you will undoubtedly find a great treasure of your own!

Chapter 11:

Living the Parisian Lifestyle: Dining, Drinks, and Nightlife

In order to truly immerse yourself in the experience of Paris, you must be open to the Parisian lifestyle, in particular the central fascination that French culture, in general, has toward good food and good wine. It is nigh impossible to say you have "done" Paris without partaking in its culture of cuisine and wine (which is nearly as ubiquitous as food itself, seconded only by coffee).

In addition to these central fascinations, there is also a burgeoning cocktail scene in Paris, conjured up by old memories of the *belle epoque* and the bohemian artist and writer scene. And, of course, there are entertainments both illicit and tame to be had in the City of Lights. Now, we must simply enjoy. The art of pleasure is a particularly French talent.

Note: because Paris is a major metropolitan hub, it is constantly in flux, with new places moving in as old places go out. Thus, this guide is mostly an overview of the best products to try and experiences to seek out, with a few specific recommendations. Always check before you travel to ensure that the places you'd like to try are still around and in the same area.

Culinary Conquest: The Supremacy of French Food

One important thing to remember about Paris is that it is the capital of France and one of the most diverse cities in all of the country. Thus, there isn't really such a thing as "Parisian" food; rather, Paris celebrates the best of French food from around the country, as well as welcoming in food traditions from immigrants who have been drawn to this city through the centuries. Still, Paris is a city obsessed with good food, from the highest to the most mundane, and you can find just about any delicacy to set your heart — and taste buds — alight. What follows here is a partial list of the food experiences that you shouldn't miss out on, with a few recommendations of specific places in which to get them.

> ➤ You absolutely must have a fresh baguette from a nearby *boulangerie*; there is no other place on earth that makes bread quite the way they do in France. Grab some cheese or charcuterie to go with it, if you like, but the bread in and of itself is a treat. You might also seek out a ham sandwich (*jambon-buerre*), one of the simplest but oh-so-amazing street treats.

- While on the subject of the bakery, you should also not miss out on a chocolate croissant. A breakfast staple in Paris, *pain au chocolat* is a buttery pastry filled with some rich, dark chocolate goes perfectly with a cup of strong coffee.

- Steak frites: one of the iconic bistro meals of Paris, this simple dish of steak with thin, crispy "French fries" is an undeniable treat. This is another reminder that, while we often think of French food as fussy and complicated, actually, they do simple and straightforward really, really well.

- Of course, any tourist knows that you should eat as much cheese as humanly possible while you are in France. It is truly a food group unto itself. However, since you are limited in how much you can eat, do go for the cheeses that are nearly impossible to find state-side (mostly for regulatory reasons): instead of going for brie—though it is far better than what you find in a typical American grocery store—choose a nice reblochon or a petit muenster, two soft and stinky cheeses that will literally ooze out of their rind at room temperature. Remember, France has literally hundreds of recognized cheeses from which to choose; do some researches before you go to figure out which is right for your tastes.

- While cheese is just as popular as a sweet for dessert, Parisians are also crazy about their sweets, and the macaron cookie may be the most popular. These marzipan-filled cookies can be found almost anywhere in Paris, though most people agree that the ones at Pierre Herme or Laudree are the best. If you're not a fun of almond flavor (or are allergic to nuts), then try a meringue cookie instead: light and airy, these just melt in your mouth.

- Another sweet tradition that is enjoyed in various ways across Europe is the hot chocolate. In Paris, it's a very different drink than what we think of in the States: it's made with real, quality dark chocolate and milk—no powdered mix or marshmallows—and is thicker, richer, and less sweet. Enjoy it with an éclair or two for one of the quintessential café experiences.

- In the wide world of street food in Paris, there are two clear winners, one a homegrown delicacy and the other an international treat: in the first category is the crepe; these are sold all over Paris in cafes and from carts, even in high-end restaurants. They can be both savory (ham and cheese is a perennial favorite) and sweet (Nutella has conquered the continent). Some suggest that Chez Alain in the Marche des Enfants Rouges makes the best savory crepe—even though the wait can be long. In the second category is the falafel, the international treat of chickpeas, spices and herbs fried to perfection and placed in a pita or eaten out of hand. L'As du Fallafel in Le Marais takes high honors for creating the best version of this in Paris.

➤ For a stand-out dish at a sit-down restaurant, you cannot go wrong with duck, whether in duck *confit* or roasted, *canard* is one of Paris's signature dishes. Richer and darker than chicken, with a depth of flavor that can only be compared to itself, duck is a gourmand's poultry dream.

➤ Another food that one cannot miss when in France generally is the oyster. The Belon oyster is renowned, though just about any variety you can get at Le Mary Celeste. If you are so inclined, please do take them raw; while you won't find cocktail sauce here (an abomination dreamt up by Americans), you might nap the oyster lightly with some mignonette sauce of champagne vinegar and chopped shallots. Better yet, don't put anything on it at all, and just enjoy the pure, briny taste of the ocean. If you can't abide them raw (or, for health reasons, must avoid them), then try them roasted with garlic butter—decadent and delicious.

➤ Speaking of garlic butter, you might just be tempted to try *escargot* while you are in Paris. Snails may not be a common occurrence in the American diet, but they are ubiquitous all over France, and chefs there have arguably figured out the best ways in which to cook them. The most popular is to broil them quickly with a topping of garlic butter and herbs.

➢ If you're looking for something hearty—let's say you're in Paris over the winter—don't miss out on one (or all) of the most renowned hearty dishes from France. Try *coq au vin*, a chicken (traditionally, a rooster) stewed in red wine with vegetables, or a choucroute garnie, a hearty baked dish of various sausages and sauerkraut (sometimes with a bit of duck confit). Or, perhaps you'd prefer a nice *beouf bourgignon*, a beef stew also cooked with red wine. Any of these will warm you up and fill you up with no problem.

➢ Finally, most people of a certain age have heard the derogatory use of the term "frog" to describe someone from France. Regardless of how the usage came to be (and that it really shouldn't be used to refer to people), there is definite truth to the fact that frogs' legs are a delicacy in France. In Paris, you can find them on many bistro menus, and they are lovely—delicate and tender, usually swimming in butter and dusted with herbs. Try them at Sacre Fleur, for one example; you'll like them.

The World of Wine and Beyond: Drinking Delights

It is a given that good food is eaten accompanied by good wine. In many places in France, wine is a constant at both lunch and dinner, though Paris is a working city so perhaps there's less of that at lunch, though it depends. If you are accustomed to drinking wine, you will find that even less expensive wines throughout the city are quite good, as it is considered so essential to living a good life. If you are not accustomed to drinking wine, give it a try (if you are able and willing) just for culture's sake. If wine isn't your thing, there are also some great places for cocktails in Paris these days. Cocktail culture is not new to Paris, though it has undergone something of a renaissance in the last decade or so, having lost traction in the abstemious 90s. Either way, be sure to imbibe responsibly; you don't want to miss out on a day in Paris because the night before was just a little too much fun.

> ➤ There are five major wine regions of France: Burgundy, Bordeaux, Champagne, Loire Valley, and Alsace. It would be good to know a little about each region and

their characteristic wines, if you wish to enjoy the best of what Paris has to offer.

- o Burgundy is most famous for its pinot noir-based (red) wines, which are delicate and nuanced. It also makes white wines with Chardonnay grapes, which are full-bodied and flavorful.
- o Bordeaux makes powerful wines, made with Cabernet Sauvignon and Merlot grapes. These can be among the most expensive wines in the world and are justifiably famous.
- o Champagne, of course, makes the only wine in the world that can legitimately be labeled "champagne." Various grapes are used in the production of champagne wines, but typically champagnes are blends of grapes (pinot meunier, pinot blanc, pinot noir) put out by the famous chateaus (houses): Dom Perignon, Taittinger, and Le Veuve Cliquot are some of the internationally known producers; however, there are a number of small producers, both relative newcomers and long-lasting stalwarts, that create champagnes with various profiles. It's worth your while, if you are a connoisseur of champagne, to look into some of these smaller

producers whose wines may not be available stateside.

- o The Loire Valley is known mostly for its white wines, particularly its Sauvignon Blanc. Lean and mineral tasting, these Loire Valley wines go very well with some iconic French foods, notably oysters.
- o Alsace wines are similar to German-style wines (the region borders Germany and has cultural characteristics in common), though tend to be a little drier than their subtly sweet German counterparts. These are white wines made from Gewürztraminer and Sylvaner.

➢ To recap, the best (or at least the most renowned) wines from Burgundy and Bordeaux are reds, with Burgundy typically being made with a single grape (pinot noir) while the more powerful Bordeaux wines are blends (cabernet sauvignon, merlot, and sometimes lesser-known grapes). Champagne is famous for, well, champagne. The Loire Valley and Alsace produce mostly white wines.

➢ Pairing wine with food is both a highly codified affair—and can be intimidating to newcomers—and an easygoing act based on personal tastes. Usually, the progression in a meal is white wines to red wines, with whites accompanying appetizers such as oysters or salads and reds accompanying main courses with meat and afterwards with cheese. If champagne is on hand, then it is typically consumed before the meal or with appetizers. However, these traditional rules have been changing for the last couple of decades, and the old idea that "you can't have red wine with fish," to name one example, has mostly fallen out of favor. Still, Parisians tend to adhere to tradition more than Americans, so if you want to fit in, you might consider sticking to these traditional rules—or, better yet, trust your sommelier (wine steward) to steer you in the right direction. Try some wines before you go to know what you like.

➢ With regard to enjoying drinks other than wine, Paris has experienced a resurgence in cocktail culture over the last decade or so; thus, there are new and expanded options for indulging in craft cocktails with lots of fancy flourishes (some of the best places to enjoy such things are mentioned in the previous chapters on different neighborhoods in Paris). If you want a truly traditional—and totally *belle epoque*—experience of Parisian cocktail culture, indulge in an absinthe, *the* drink of the bohemian set at the end of the 19th and beginning of the 20th centuries. Made from wormwood and other botanicals, "the green fairy" is surrounded by myth and ritual; it's not to everyone's taste—it can be quite bitter and strong—but it is a quintessentially Parisian pastime. Try Cantada II, if you're interested, which has nearly 70 varieties to choose from.

➤ For another blast of the past, head out to Harry's Bar in the Opera district. This legendary bar is expensive but rife with history and their traditional Bloody Mary still can't be beat. If you prefer something on the sweeter side, try the Side Car.

➤ While Paris, and France in general, isn't thought to be much of a beer culture, there is certainly that tradition, as well. Brasseries—casual restaurants that serve hearty food and good beer—populate all corners of France. One of the best in Paris is Brasserie La Goutte d'Or, which serves its own microbrews. Microbrewery culture came late to Paris, but in recent years, it has been blossoming. If you're interested in beer, do some searching for what's new and trending.

Let Us Entertain You: Paris Nightlife

From the public dances and outdoor concerts to the many theaters and cabarets, Paris has always had a vigorous and exciting nightlife scene. There are many different styles of nightlife throughout the city, and you will inevitably find something here that is right for you. The following ideas not only list the kinds of nightlife activities you might find in Paris, but also the atmosphere of nightlife culture in different areas of the city. This should steer you in the right direction, once you're ready to get out and about in the City of Lights.

> ➢ Le Marais is the place to see and be seen it is younger, trendier, and louder than most of the other neighborhoods in Paris after dark. It is also LGBTQ friendly with a number of gay clubs in the area. The Bastille locale is also similar.

> ➢ The Champs-Elysees area, in stark contrast, is less local and more tourist-oriented, as well as being much more expensive and formal. If you do head out here for a night on the town, dress in your Paris finest for best results.

> ➢ Montmartre has always been a draw for nightlife, what with the famous Moulin Rouge and other cabarets. This is also why it is often branded as seedy or potentially

dangerous, especially in the Pigalle area, though that is perhaps exaggerated, as long as you exercise reasonable caution. In fact, Montmartre is the neighborhood in which you might get the most balanced mix of tourists and locals alike.

➤ Belleville is another neighborhood in which nightlife flourishes, albeit of a different sort. The birthplace of legendary singer, Edith Piaf, Belleville is a working-class area of Paris with pubs and clubs welcoming all. Not many tourists venture here, as of yet.

➤ The Latin Quarter attracts a bohemian population—and lots of students—and has a good number of fun bars and music venues, including the Le Caveau de la Huchette which has been a jazz bar since the end of the World War II.

Chapter 12:

Beyond the City: Off the Beaten Path

While Paris proper has endless amounts of entertainment, history, art, and culture to offer, there are things to do and see beyond the city limits. Taking a day trip outside the city offers a break from the hustle and bustle (in some cases), as well as allows you the experience of seeing the French countryside, at least in a partial way.

Some of these activities can be accessed via tour buses that regularly leave the city for certain famous sites (such as Versailles), while others might encourage you to rent a car and spend a little time navigating France on your own. If you have enough time while you are visiting the famed City of Lights, you might consider one of the following destinations to round out your trip.

> ➢ Obviously, the Palace of Versailles is the most renowned of the side trips from Paris. In fact, this visit is considered by most travel experts to be a mere extension of your trip to Paris—that is, essential for any in-depth experience of the capital of France. This elaborate (some might say decadent) symbol of the doomed French aristocracy survived the ravages of the Revolution and its aftermath—perhaps because it was simply too beautiful to destroy. Built by the Sun King, Louis XIV, the palace was home to monarchs up until the ill-fated Louis XVI and his infamous wife, Marie Antoinette, fell to the guillotine. Among its many charms is the renowned Hall of Mirrors, with its many arched mirrors and tall windows; at the time of its construction, mirrors were still a rare and luxurious commodity, so this was a display not only of beauty but also of wealth and power. The palace's many gardens are also famous for their landscaped beauty, especially

in spring, and Marie Antoinette's private quarters, Le Petit Trianon, is also open to visitors. Our enduring fascination with this decadent and doomed queen heightens the pleasure of a visit to Versailles.

- o You can take the RER-C, a commuter train line, out to Versailles, rather than having to rent a car or hire a driver. The station stop is Versailles-Rive Gauche and has signs directing tourists to the entrance of the palace. This is a full day's trip, with the two-hour round-trip commute combined with the usually crowded entrance and the large ground to cover (each of the three main attractions—the Chateau itself, the gardens, and Le Petit Trianon—will take up about one and a half hours).

- ➢ If you're really into palaces, or if Versailles seems too crowded for you, you might consider the less popular—though some argue even more beautiful—Chateau Vaux-le-Vicomte. It has served as a set for any number of period films set in pre-revolutionary France and was the source of inspiration for writers such as Moliere. It also has luxurious gardens with statuary and fountains in abundance.

- You can take the RER-D, another commuter train line, out to Melun. From there, you take a free shuttlebus to and from the Chateau.

➤ Yet another royal residence is worth a day trip from Paris: the Fontainebleu Palace and Park was once a retreat of the aristocracy from the 13th century to the Revolution. Located near the historic town of Barbizon, the Fontainebleu is a destination for nature lovers, with its miles of hiking trails and forested land. Bring a picnic and enjoy being out in nature after perusing the medieval castle.

- There is a regional train line out of the Gare de Lyon in Paris—the SNCF line—which will take you to Fontainebleu-Avon. From there, you can walk to the palace. In fact, be prepared for a lot of walking if you decide to tackle this day trip; the park and forest are the biggest draws here.

➤ About an hour's drive away from Paris, you can find the home of internationally beloved French painter, Claude Monet. His famous paintings of garden scenes often came directly out of his own backyard: his gardens are intricately designed masterworks of nature, with the renowned water lily ponds and Japanese-influenced style. It is a must-see for any dedicated fan of Monet, if for nothing else than to see the inspiration behind some of his most famous paintings. The house itself is also open to the public and contains a number of his own works and other memorabilia.

- o The house and gardens are located in Giverny and can be reached by train and shuttle. Take the train to Vernon (from the Gare Saint-Lazare station) where shuttle buses will take you on to Giverny. Travel time is about two hours round trip, and you want to give yourself at least two hours there, but it can be done in half a day if the crowds aren't too bad. The best time to go is in the spring, when the gardens are in full bloom.

- ➢ If you are a dedicated fan of gothic architecture and medieval history, then the Saint-Denis Cathedral Basilica is worth a quick trip from Paris. Accessible by Metro 13, the small town of Saint-Denis is really just a working-class suburb of Paris, but it houses a world class cathedral and necropolis. The gothic architecture of Saint-Denis may not be as famous as that of Notre Dame, though it is still stunning. Housed within the Basilica is a necropolis of famous kings, queens, and other royal figures lying in repose; these tributes to royalty are unusual in a country that cherishes its democratic revolution, so this is one of the few places, besides Versailles, where you can see that royal past. It is also said to be the burial place of Saint Denis himself, as well as the location of one of Joan of Arc's pilgrimages.

- o On a sunny day, the stained glass really allows the cathedral to shine—literally. Follow Metro 13 to the Saint-Denis stop. It's best to visit during the day as it can be a little rough at night.

➢ Lest we not forget, the second most famous cathedral in France—a nation packed with them—is the wonderful Chartres Cathedral, the only true rival to Notre Dame in the national imagination. About an hour away from Paris, this magnificent medieval cathedral was under construction just a couple of decades after Notre Dame, in 1190, and finished before it, in 1220. Chartres also has the dramatic flying buttresses and gorgeous stained glass. Because of its location, it has been remarkably well-preserved, with much of the original material still in play. Its rounded turrets are distinctive, and this site was declared a World Heritage Site by UNESCO.

- There are numerous trains out of Paris to Chartre because of its enduring popularity, particularly during Catholic holidays (when it will be inevitably crowded). If you go when the weather is nice, the views of the stained-glass windows are unparalleled.

- Another UNESCO World Heritage site, the preserved medieval village of Provins is a fascinating short trip from Paris. This is where the products from the famed Silk Road ended up, the spices and silks and other exotic fare where bartered on the streets of this small town. It still boasts its original stone fortifications and has inspired many writers down through the years, including Victor Hugo, with its medieval charm. There are medieval festivals throughout the year; if you are thinking about taking a trip, be sure to check the local web site for information on what festivals or theatrical productions are playing during your visit, so you can plan accordingly.

  - The best way to get there is by taking the SCNF regional train to Provins; it leaves via the Gare de l'Est. Allow two hours for round trip travel.

➢ If you are a wine connoisseur, then a day trip to the famed region of Champagne may be on your itinerary. A little more than an hour away from Paris, the towns and cellars of the region beckon with their world-renowned alcoholic beverage. As any connoisseur is well aware, this is the only region in the world from which authentic champagne can come, and it is well worth a trip to the region to check out the numerous chateaus that have been operating for hundreds of years. In particular, the town of Reims is another UNESCO World Heritage site and home to such famed vintners as Dom Perignon and Taittinger. Not only will you get to taste some world class wines, but you will also learn about the history of the region and the families here who made this one of the most economically significant regions in all of Europe.

   o You can take a SCNF train from Paris to visit the region, though if you wish to travel amongst the chateaus, your best bet is to rent a car—and, of course, have a designated driver.

➢ Finally, if you are both a food and a wine connoisseur and have enough time in your trip for a weekend getaway from the city, you might consider a trip to Burgundy. This is the home of some of France's finest foods and wines, with the cities of Beaune and Dijon perhaps being the most popular to visit. Beaune boasts some of the most prestigious wine cellars in all of France, while Dijon is, of course, the birthplace of the quintessentially French mustard. If you do decide to undertake this trip, be sure to do some research on where to stay a night or two and what chateaus are open when. There are numerous private tour companies who will also plan a trip for you.

- o Accessible by high-speed trains out of Paris, Burgundy is about a two-hour trip, which is why it's probably more of a weekend jaunt. Again, renting a car (or going with a private tour company) is perhaps the best way to get the most out of a visit here.

Chapter 13:

Practical Considerations: Money, Transportation, and a Checklist for the First-Timer

Now that you're ready to go to Paris and have your favorite sites already in mind, it's time to start thinking about the practical considerations. This chapter should help you with a variety of basic information that gets you ready for your actual trip, from planning and booking to how to exchange money and how to get around. There are also some tips about how to navigate your tourist experience, some advice on potential emergencies, and some ideas on what to bring back. The following checklist should have you well prepared to book your trip and have the experience of a lifetime.

> ➤ Obviously, you will want to give yourself time to plan your trip. The first order of business that you must take care of is getting a passport, if you don't already have one. This process can take up to two months, so plan accordingly.

> ➤ When you have your passport, you'll need to decide when to go; this will depend on many factors, not least

of which will be your budget and your time. See Chapter 2 for more information on when to go to Paris and what to do in any season.

- If you decide to go during the height of tourist season (May and June, September and October are the busiest), then you must be sure to book well in advance in order to get the optimal hotel, restaurant and entertainment reservations, and so on.

- You want to make other reservations in advance, as well, such as train tickets and car rentals if you plan on making day trips from the city. You should also look into getting a Paris Museum Pass, which allows entry into all of the city's major museums and some other attractions (and will also allow you to skip most long lines), before you go. These are available in two-, four-, or six-day increments. You can arrange to have it ready for pick up at your hotel. Finally, consider booking an entrance time at the Eiffel Tower before you leave, as well.

- With regard to money, Paris uses the euro, and the exchange rate fluctuates, of course (the web site **www.oanda.com** has the latest information about exchange rates). It is a good idea to have some euros with you before you leave, if you can find a good rate, and it is always better to exchange larger amounts than continue to pull out smaller amounts of cash—there are always fees associated with exchanging currency. Check with your bank and credit card companies to see how that works and be sure to let them know that you will be overseas so that your cards aren't cut off for suspected fraud.

➤ Paris is generally very safe, but you do want to be aware of your valuables and belongings in crowded touristy areas. Most hotels have a safe where you can keep valuables while you are out of the room. When moving about in the city, keep your money close to your person, in the form of a money belt or a purse slung across the chest. Never put valuables or money in a backpack— that's too easy to lose track of.

➤ When you arrive in Paris, you will be at one of the terminals of Charles de Gaulle airport, where there are tourist information kiosks and banks, as well as food and drink options. It's a good idea to know in advance how you will get from the airport to your hotel: you can take a taxi (the most expensive option); you can take a bus (there are a couple of options depending on where your hotel is located); you can take a train (cheap but a little complicated); or you can find out if your hotel has an airport van, which shuttle visitors to and from the airport. This last option is both economical and simple, though you will sometimes have to wait a while for the next one to arrive.

- Most hotels will have a detailed city map for free, so don't worry about purchasing one (or invest in a good guidebook with a detachable map). The concierge is also a valuable source of information, such as how to get around and use the Metro, as well as giving recommendations for local restaurants and entertainment. If you are staying in an area that caters to tourists, most people you encounter will speak some English, though it is a good idea to have some handy French phrases at the ready, just in case: *bonjour* (good day) is a standard greeting, while *s'il vous plait* means please and *merci* means thank you. You can always immediately ask, *parlez vous anglais?* To see if someone speaks English.

- Remember that France uses the 24-hour clock, so 6.00 in the morning is 6.00 a.m., but 6.00 in the evening is 18.00 p.m. Paris is six to nine hours ahead of American time (from East coast to West). Also note that dates are written European style, with day/month/year, so Christmas would be rendered 25/12/2020.

- Another important detail to note is that Paris, like most of Europe, uses the 220 volt electrical system (in the U.S., it is 110 volts); thus, if you plan to use devices that plug in (phone, tablet, or laptop charger; hair dryer; curling iron, etc.), you will need an adapter plug. Newer devices no longer need a converter, typically speaking, but check to be sure.

- ➢ Some random bits of information to help with potential confusion: decimals and commas are used differently in Europe, so money will be rendered 2,50 and distance will be written 1.768 kilometers. Paris uses the metric system and measures temperature with Celsius rather than Fahrenheit. Thus, to roughly convert Celsius to Fahrenheit, double the number and add 30: so, if it's 21 degrees Celsius, then it would be roughly 70 degrees Fahrenheit.

- ➢ The neighborhood stores labeled *tabacs* are handy for the tourist in that they sell some Metro tickets, stamps, and phone cards.

- ➢ The best way to get around Paris is to use the Metro: they are efficient and ubiquitous throughout the city. Study a map of the Metro before you go, so you know where the stop nearest your hotel is; most stops near major attractions are named after the attraction so that makes figuring out where to go simpler. You have the option of buying what is called a *carnet* of Metro tickets, which offers value: these tickets don't expire, they can be shared, and they are cheaper than buying single tickets at a time.

➤ The Metro is organized by color and each different line is known by the name of its end destination, so the signs you see will say "direction: La Defense," for example. Keep your ticket in case you are asked to show it at your stop. If you need to transfer from one line to another, follow the orange *correspondence* (connection) signs, and when you reach your destination, follow the blue-and-white *sortie* (exit) signs. It takes a bit of getting used to, but the Metro is fairly simple to use. If you've ever used the Metro in Washington, DC, then you'll have no trouble; DC's subway was modeled on Paris.

➤ There is also a RER train line that works pretty much like the Metro but designed for longer trips within the city with fewer stops. Tickets are interchangeable.

➤ Paris also has a lauded bus system, and it works just as buses do everywhere else. Paris's buses have a reputation for being efficient and on time. Some people find the bus system a little more complicated to use than the Metro, while others find the Metro to be confusing. Just study routes ahead of time, and you should have no problem.

➤ Finally, there are always taxis and Uber: taxis are expensive, of course, in comparison to the Metro and the bus, while Uber is a ride at your own risk scenario. Uber is very active in Paris, though not all Parisians are happy about this, and cheaper certainly than taxis though still not as economical as the Metro or bus. You will also need to have some workable French in most instances.

➢ Remember that on the first Sunday of the month, some museums are free: The Louvre, the Orsay, Cluny, Rodin, and Pompidou Center. If you invested in a Paris Museum Pass—which you really should do—then you don't need the freebie and should avoid the museums on these days, as they are very crowded. Most churches and parks are free. Some attractions offer reduced prices if you go late in the day, including The Louvre.

➢ Paris is generally a very safe city. The only thing most tourists should be aware of is pickpockets around major sites. Just be careful and aware, and you should be fine. If something is stolen or if you are assaulted, you can call the number 17 for English-speaking assistance. If you have a medical emergency, dial 15 for an ambulance. For minor health issues, check with your concierge or drop into a local pharmacy (these all have green crosses on the signs) where there are always professionals who can help you find medication or first aid.

➢ Last, you will obviously want to bring back some souvenirs for yourself and for your loved ones. Be sure to check with the latest FAA rules about what passengers can bring on planes or in luggage/carry-ons with them. With regard to food products, be aware that you cannot bring back most produce and meat. You can bring back cheese, but only hard and semi-soft cheeses (no rebolochon, alas), and charcuterie like salami. You can also bring back wine packed in your suitcase, though if you are buying wine, it can be well worth it to buy a case or two and have it shipped back to your house; most chateaus and reputable wine shops will be happy to do this for you. Check out all the rules at U.S. Customs and Border Protection if you have questions about something you want to bring back.

Conclusion

Now that you have learned just about everything a tourist needs to know about Paris, it is time to get your bags packed and your itinerary planned. Be sure to keep a running checklist of everything a knowledgeable tourist could ever want to see, from the Eiffel Tower to the Louvre and on to Notre Dame and beyond, you are prepared to visit all of this and more. Take a stroll through Le Marais and enjoy the nightlife in Montmartre. Spend a day in the Latin Quarter, shopping for literary souvenirs and enjoying ethnic bites. Visit a market or two, and make reservations at a famous restaurant, experiences being the best souvenirs there are.

Don't forget to travel with an open mind and open heart: Paris is famously filled with the unexpected and the unexplored. Eat and drink like a Parisian, and celebrate the singular history of this marvelous city, the center of France and a beacon of light throughout Europe. The City of Lights waits only for you to arrive.

Appendix: Maps

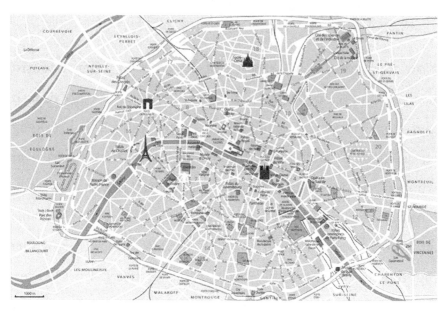

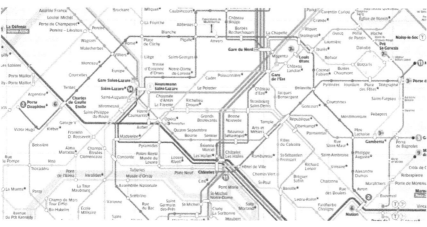

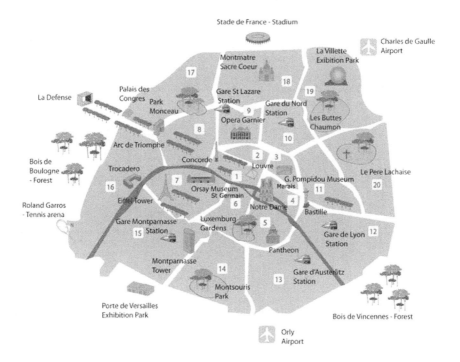

Stade de France - Stadium

Charles de Gaulle Airport

La Villette Exibition Park

Montmatre Sacre Coeur

17

18

19

La Defense

Palais des Congres

Park Monceau

Gare St Lazare Station

Gare du Nord Station

Opera Garnier

9

Les Buttes Chaumon

8

10

Arc de Triomphe

Concorde

2 3

Louvre

Le Pere Lachaise

Bois de Boulogne - Forest

Trocadero

1

G. Pompidou Museum

Marais

20

16

7

Orsay Museum

St Germain

11

Roland Garros - Tennis arena

Eiffel Tower

6

Notre Dame

4

Bastille

Gare Montparnasse Station

15

Luxemburg Gardens

5

Gare de Lyon Station

12

Montparnasse Tower

14

Pantheon

Gare d'Austerlitz Station

13

Montsouris Park

Porte de Versailles Exhibition Park

Bois de Vincennes - Forest

Orly Airport

Made in the USA
Monee, IL
20 August 2021